Deliver Me From Evil

Deliver Me From Evil

A SADISTIC FOSTER MOTHER, A CHILDHOOD TORN APART

ALLOMA GILBERT

With Corinne Sweet

PAN BOOKS

First published 2008 by Pan Books
an imprint of Pan Macmillan Ltd
Pan Macmillan, 20 New Wharf Road, London N1 9RR
Basingstoke and Oxford
Associated companies throughout the world
www.panmacmillan.com

ISBN 978-0-330-45731-6

9 8 7 6 5 4 3 2 1

A CIP catalogue record for this book is available from the British Library.

Typeset by Andrew Barker Information Design
Printed and bound in Great Britain by
Mackays of Chatham plc, Chatham, Kent

For my beautiful daughter

Contents

Author's Note

In March 2007 I stood up in court to testify against Eunice Spry, to describe publicly for the first time the horrific abuse she put me through. A court order protected my identity and I was simply known as Child B.

It is my choice to waive anonymity and write now under my real name. The last thing I want to do is cause any more pain to the other children still living who suffered at Eunice Spry's hands for so many years. For that reason I am not using their real names in this book. And although I cannot tell my story without telling theirs to some extent, I have tried not to go beyond the information already given in court.

In fact, some of what came out in court from their testimony was unknown to me before – Eunice did her best to keep us divided and although we lived together we did not share everything. So this is my story about my childhood; their experiences will be slightly different.

I am proud of all of us, for surviving and making new lives for ourselves. We have a long way to go yet but I have faith that we will in the end be able to put the past firmly behind us. Writing this book was an important step on the road to recovery for me. Eunice terrorized us into silence for many years – now I have found my voice at last.

CHAPTER 1: *Finding My Voice*

It's her eyes. I can't bear to see her eyes. A hard, dead grey, they will bore into me, into my very soul, and then I'll be lost. I know I'll buckle. I'll believe her vile words as she spits them at me, stabbing me through the heart with every accusation.

'You are evil scum. You're the Devil's child. You have to be taught a lesson that you'll never, ever forget.'

I've stopped breathing. I gulp in air and everything suddenly comes into focus. The black shiny car I'm trying desperately to disappear into the back of pulls into Avis Car Hire. Thank goodness for the tinted windows. Although it's dim in the garage forecourt, I see a couple of people I recognize waiting for us. Then the door opens slowly. I'm relieved when a warm, friendly face appears and Detective Constable (DC) Victoria Martell slides in beside me, while a male officer gets in the front.

The DC is dressed in a smart black suit and shoes – she always looks very professional, but glamorous. There's a waft of perfume as she turns her attractive face, framed by long, dark hair, and touches my hand lightly. 'How're you doing, Alloma?'

I'm so glad she's there. I'm beginning to breathe more easily again. I swallow hard and try to speak, but I can't get the words out. My tongue feels like it's a large sponge and my stomach starts churning. I awoke at dawn after a restless night of fitful, nightmare-filled sleep and couldn't eat breakfast. Now my stomach gurgles – I'm not hungry, but I somehow feel sick and empty at the same time.

To distract myself I start fiddling with my pretty bead bracelet as feelings of panic begin to bubble up through my body. I like the feel of the smooth chunks of coloured glass as they roll between my nervous fingers. *I don't know if I can go through with this.* I steal a glance at DC Martell's face as the car's engine purrs into life and we glide into Bristol's busy morning traffic. She looks very determined, while I feel extremely wobbly inside.

Pink blossom hangs in heavy clusters on the trees and there are masses of fresh green leaves: spring has come early. I love to see nature coming into its own, bursting with new life. This time of year really thrills me; I'd like to be out in my back garden now, enjoying the fresh air and the pretty spring flowers. More than anything I'd like to be holding my beautiful little daughter, Ivy, in my arms and spinning her around in the park, or listening to her delighted giggles as she strokes one of our six cats.

In fact, I'd rather be anywhere, doing anything, right now, other than heading for a grim day in court.

'You look nice, Alloma, very smart.' DC Martell is smiling encouragingly, as the car nudges through heavy traffic. 'Glad you were able to borrow some cash and get to the shops.'

I look down to my legs, clad in unfamiliar smart brown trousers. I see the edges of my crisp fawn jacket and clean white shirt cuffs. A formal style, so unlike my usual casual jeans and glittery T-shirts, the only concession to the 'real me' being my long, sparkly 'gypsy' earrings. My curly black hair is tamed into a half ponytail and I fiddle with the hairband. I try to breathe more deeply, as I learned to when I had Ivy, but I just can't keep still.

Although DC Martell's is a reassuring presence beside me, I can still remember scrawny hands around my throat, trying to stop me from speaking out, squeezing the life out of me to 'teach me a lesson'. Remembering that my foster mother, Eunice Spry – the owner of those terrifying hands – is safely in police custody, I finally find my voice, even though it's a bit croaky and dry. 'Thanks, Victoria. But are you really sure there'll be a screen?'

DC Martell's face softens. 'I'm sure, Alloma. She'll be brought into court after you've arrived, so you really won't see her face. I promise.'

I nod slowly, trying to take this in. *God I hope you're right*, I think, because if she can see me, she can get me. The minute

I'm skewered by her gaze I'll think I'm bad. Dirty. Evil. It happens in an instant. I can't hold onto myself in her presence. The minute she's anywhere near I feel I'm a terrible person.

'Don't forget, you gave evidence to me for your statement on video, so you won't have to go through all that painful detail again, ' the DC says.

How could I forget? *But she'll be there*, I think. *She'll know.* She'll be staring at me with hatred, through the screen, trying to psych me out. She's very good at that. And when she hears me speak, she'll call me a liar, she'll throw everything back at me. She'll never, ever forgive me, that's for sure. I imagine those steely eyes coming towards me, bearing down on me with calculating malice. Like they have a thousand times since I was small. I feel myself shudder.

'Are you sure you're OK, Alloma? You're white as a sheet.'

DC Martell leans towards me, concerned. My careful make-up job clearly doesn't conceal everything. I can't speak I'm so terrified. Words often fail me when I'm scared, especially as I've been forcefully taught to be quiet and not speak, most of the time.

Then suddenly we are gliding through a gate and drawing up to the back entrance of an imposing Regency-style building: Bristol Crown Court. DC Martell has already told me that we need to avoid the crowds of photographers and reporters gathered at the front, but the officer in the front seat turns and explains they're being extra careful because my case is big – as big as the Fred West case was, in nearby Gloucester.

This freaks me out. *I didn't die,* I think. *It wasn't that bad.* No one actually died because of Eunice's treatment, although we often thought we would.

The car comes to a halt and the door swings open. DC Martell hops out and shepherds me towards some steps where we're swept up by officials in uniform. Once inside, I'm frisked by security (I set the beepers off with my metal buckle and jewellery) then ushered into a little box room where I have to read through my long statement again. I'm very nervous about being cross-examined and, although the statement is all my own words, I fear I'll forget to say something, or maybe even keel over and die with fright.

The brusque court official tells me that I mustn't discuss my statement with anyone. Then she brings me a cup of tea and I ask for loads of sugar – I need the energy as I have not eaten yet. I'm warned bluntly that I might have to wait all morning for my turn. To be honest, I don't care if it never comes as I dread being questioned and having to talk in front of so many strange and official-looking people. But I don't like being shut in this little box room either, so it needs to start soon.

After so many years of suffering in silence – since I was six and a half, when Eunice first took me over – I suppose another few hours won't make a huge difference. I just feel as though I am on a precipice, looking down into an abyss. There's absolutely no way back and only one way forward, but

I don't know yet if I'm brave enough to take it. What's more, now that I'm in the middle of this huge legal process, everything is out of my control.

All I can do is try to keep going, stay calm and tell the truth. At least, that's the theory; that's what I've been told to do by DC Martell and others who believe me. And there are more witnesses. In particular, two young adults who suffered as I did and who are telling their stories, too. The real issue is whether or not other people – in this case, a jury of twelve complete strangers – will believe our extraordinary story.

Reading through the pages of my statement I begin to feel extremely sad. The wording is childlike even though I was nineteen when I wrote it. I realize, for the first time, just how naive I was compared to other teenagers. The events my statement describes truly feel like a lifetime ago now, as I sit in my nice new clothes, twenty-one years of age – and a mother of a youngster myself – about to give evidence at a major trial, like a proper grown-up.

The door opens. 'It's time,' says the court official. I straighten my clothes and hair nervously as I try to stand up, but my legs have suddenly turned to jelly. A witness support officer leads me along the corridor to the lift that will take me up to the courtroom. In the lift I fiddle with my bracelet while my heart hammers in my chest so loudly that I'm sure everyone will hear it.

The doors open. I take a deep breath. *This is it.*

CHAPTER 2: *Bright Eyes*

As a little girl I knew absolutely that my parents loved me. That security is the greatest gift you can give a child and is something most of us are lucky enough to take for granted. I don't. I am grateful to my mum and dad for showing me warmth and affection, for every hug and kiss and kind word, for giving me six years free from fear – because I know what it is like when all of that is taken away and replaced by extreme cruelty. Without the memory of being loved once, I think I might not have survived my years with Eunice Spry.

It was only during the writing of this book that I really started to understand how Eunice managed to take over my life so completely. I look back at the moments – each one small in itself – that brought her closer to my family and wish passionately that I could go back in time and change them. I am sure my parents wish the same. One thing I do know is that my parents always tried to do their best for me. In the end, they too were Eunice's victims.

*

I was born on 14 May 1985 in Cheltenham, a genteel market town in the south-west of England. I was named Alloma Lesley Gilbert – Alloma was a name from a book my mum had loved, about mythical people and fairies; she was into anything mystical. Her family had Romany heritage, hailing originally from Ireland. I'm told they had even lived in a gypsy caravan at one time, which sounds romantic and colourful, but nothing like the reality of my mum's life. She grew up in Bolton, Lancashire, and had a violent upbringing, being abused by her own mother. She ran away as a teenager and gradually lost touch with everyone and everything she had known. Her mum is now dead and I never met any other members of her family, except for a distant cousin. The rest, I suppose, live all over the place; I'd love to be able to trace them one day.

My dad had a more settled childhood, living with his parents in their council bungalow on the outskirts of Cheltenham. But he had a rebellious streak and, like many teenagers, experimented with drugs, much to the disapproval of his parents.

Mum and Dad met when they were both fifteen at a club in London in the early psychedelic seventies and fell wildly in love. Mum was pretty, with cascades of curly dark hair and blue eyes. She was extremely artistic, a free spirit, a seeker, looking to start a new life away from her painful home experiences.

Dad was an attractive young man, with his dark hair and

brown eyes, and also something of a wild child. I suppose when they met they must have felt like kindred spirits. Although they were very young to start a relationship, their feelings for each other didn't change and my dad soon brought my mum to Cheltenham to live with him and his parents.

This is where I come in. Mum had a stillborn child before I was born, which affected her deeply. It took another five years from then for my parents to conceive, so I can only imagine that I was a wanted child. We all lived with Nan in her bungalow until my granddad died when I was just a year old. Although I can't remember him, my granddad left me one important legacy: the name 'Bright Eyes' which everyone used to call me at home.

The first year of my life was quite difficult for my parents. My mum was poorly after my birth, and she and my dad had to get used to the responsibility of a new baby who cried, needed feeding, dressing and generally looking after. Losing my granddad put further strain on all of the adults.

To make matters worse, I was born with a cleft palate – a small hole in the roof of my mouth, near the back, which meant food went up my nose and was hard to swallow. Luckily, I didn't have a harelip, which so often occurs with a cleft palate, but I still had to have an operation when I was about eighteen months old. I don't remember going to hospital, but the surgery must have been complicated as I'm told it took me about a month to get over it.

Around the same time, my mum had to have a gall-bladder operation; the authorities believed my dad and elderly nan would not be able to cope with my particular needs, especially with Mum recovering from her own surgery. Gloucestershire Social Services decided, therefore, that foster care was needed for me. They had a carer on their books who seemed perfect for the job: Eunice Spry.

When I think of my mum and dad at this time it's as a kind of grown-up Hansel and Gretel, lost in the dark and bewildering woods of parenthood, unable to find their way. Along comes Eunice, then about forty-two years old, no doubt looking kindly and respectable in sensible clothes, a mother of two and seemingly full of common sense. Maybe her strait-laced religious nature – she was a devout Jehovah's Witness at the time – made her seem particularly reassuring.

Eunice always seemed to have time for babies and treated them fairly well, so as I was a poor mite with 'bright eyes' and a cleft palate, maybe I moved her heart at that first, fateful meeting? Had my parents known then what they know now, I am sure they would have slammed the door firmly shut and bolted it hard against the apparently caring woman who would go on to perpetrate the most unthinkable harm.

I have no memory of that first stay with Eunice Spry. I know that I moved into her house at 24 George Dowty Drive in Tewkesbury, a forty-minute drive from Cheltenham, for a month. At around one and a half I would have been toddling about and 'into everything' like any young, intelligent child. My parents and nan missed out on my recovery from surgery and some of my first exploratory moves towards independence in the world.

Eunice had two daughters of her own living with her at that time – the youngest was in her late teens, the oldest, Judith, was in her early twenties – and she was still married to her first husband, who apparently adored her. They must have seemed like a nice, normal family. Indeed, Eunice had already been allowed by Gloucestershire Social Services to adopt her first girl, Charlotte, when she was a baby. She was just three when I went to stay.

After a month I was returned to my parents. I wonder now what Eunice thought of our little family: whether we were just one of many she encountered as a foster mother, or whether, looking at my vulnerable parents, she had some inkling she would see us again.

She did contact my parents six months later for a reference to give to Gloucestershire Social Services so she could foster, and later adopt, another little girl called Sarah.

Once I was back in the bungalow my parents and nan decided they needed more space. After all, although Mum and Dad had never married we were a family. They applied to the council for a bigger place and, when I was about two and a half, we all moved into a three-bedroom semi-detached terraced house in a quiet, leafy road in Cheltenham. It was a typical fifties-style pebble-dashed council house, with a side entrance and a strip of scrubby garden at the back.

My first memory of our new house was my third birthday party. It had a clown theme, with balloons and clown faces decorating the dining room. I distinctly remember hanging onto the edges of a dark mahogany table and looking up with wonder at my fabulous clown cake.

Our living room looked onto the street and had a small TV in one corner. I'd sit on the floor in front of it and watch *Sesame Street* and *Finger Mouse*, totally absorbed in their worlds of fantasy and make-believe. I loved the songs and larger-than-life characters and would happily watch for hours on end. My mum would lie or sit on the sofa that ran along the back wall and across double doors which led to the largely unused dining room. Two armchairs were squashed in quite close together – one nearer the door, which my dad sat in, the other near the window, which I often used.

In the hall, which ran from the front door, past the stairs and on to the kitchen, there was a large, threadbare green sofa. I think it was a cast-off that no one had got around to moving out of the house. It blocked the bottom of the stairs and when I was little I couldn't get past it, so I had to be lifted over. In fact, at one time there was a mouse's nest in it and at night you could hear the sound of chewing on the stairs, a hollow, grating sound, which I found quite scary. I'd lie awake at night, listening, as all sorts of strange images ran through my mind. It was very spooky, knowing that a little animal was gnawing away downstairs, just a short distance away.

There was a picture on the wall at the bottom of the stairs – it was of the coast and had an old brown frame and as it was one of the few pictures in the house, I would sit on the stairs or play on the sofa and gaze at it. The hall sofa blocked the front door, too, so we could never use it. Instead, we had to go down a side passage with a corrugated plastic roof outside the house and come in through the back door. I took it for granted that we would always come in round the back and through the kitchen.

I have random memories of my parents from those early days in our new family home. My dad would pick me up and lift me above his head and zoom me around, calling me 'his little aeroplane'. I loved it and would giggle madly as he did so. He was quite physically playful back then – moments like that were great. I really felt he loved me, as did my mum – although she was less demonstrative.

Dad would sometimes read me bedtime stories, bringing the books to life. But once he'd tucked me in and gone downstairs, I'd often find I wasn't sleepy and would get back out of bed, pretending to be a cat, a dog or a fox, scooting around on all fours in the dark. After several trips upstairs to try and settle me, Dad would eventually get annoyed and shout, 'Get back in bed and stay there'. But before long I'd be meowing my way around the room again, as though sniffing at flowers or chasing butterflies. My imagination would take over as it always did.

I also have a vague memory of cooking with my mum one day in the kitchen, making something like spaghetti Bolognese, using a jar of sauce. I was stirring something and, for a laugh, my dad gave me a chilli pepper to see my reaction. I can still remember the unbearably searing hot sensation and my dad scooping me up and rushing me to the bathroom for water to cool my burning mouth.

I can see Mum hanging out washing on a line in what seemed like a massive garden. It was cultivated at one point, but soon became overgrown, providing me with a mysteriously lush place in which to explore and play my imaginary games. I could amuse myself with the slightest things: following a butterfly, talking to a cat or watching the neighbour's daughter, Penny, play with her pet chihuahua – I thought it was such a funny little thing.

My parents would take me to Pitville Park in Cheltenham, which I loved as there were rabbits, peacocks and pheasants there. We'd feed bread to the birds and ducks and Dad would pick clover buds for the rabbits. I loved the bunnies with their twitchy noses and was captivated by the peacocks' plumage, believing my dad when he told me the patterns on their feathers were real eyes. I hated the sound of the parrots squawking, so Dad would take me past their cages quickly and go on to the swings and roundabouts. I'd rock back and forth on a coloured horse whose body was fixed to a large coiled spring, while Dad said, 'Whoop, giddyup, horsey, to the fair. What will we find when we get there?'

I also have vivid memories of Mum picking roses in the park and taking them home to dry the petals. I can still hear her singing as she bent down to pick each one. At home she'd take them apart carefully, dry them on newspaper in the airing cupboard, and then blend them with aromatic oils to make pot pourri. Mum liked to make things and enjoyed creative pursuits like needlework and collage. We kept lots of art magazines in large black plastic bags in the kitchen and Mum loved to flick through them. I'd spend hours staring at the 'How to draw' articles, fascinated by them.

The house was generally untidy but my parents would have huge clear-ups every so often and try to make things nice, especially at Christmas, after which it would almost immediately start to deteriorate again, getting increasingly messy.

Mum and Dad found it difficult to cope with running a house and looking after me. My mum's fragile health was part of the reason our home life was sometimes chaotic. But also to blame was my parents' teenage experimentation with drugs. They knew they had a problem and, bravely, sought help when I was very young. They would go daily to a local drug re-habilitation centre, often taking me with them. They'd manage to make it a fun outing, treating me to a hot lunch in the canteen and then going to the park on the way home.

As things got harder at home I began to retreat into myself, playing alone more and more. I spent a lot of the time in my bedroom or in the garden, making up stories, characters or songs in my head. With my vivid imagination I could be alone for hours, keeping myself amused. I'd hang out of the bathroom window upstairs and play with the wood lice that lived in the rotten window frame, chattering away to them as though they were my friends.

We had a cat at one time, called Smeagol (named after the character in *The Lord of the Rings*). I adored her and was so excited when she had kittens – until a lady came and took them away, saying they would go to a better home. Then someone else came along and took Smeagol away, saying she ought to go to a better home, too. I was so upset, but my parents just said, 'Oh, the nice lady has taken them to a nicer house,' and that was that.

Then, when I was about four, something happened that devastated me, and which I didn't understand at all at the time.

One morning I saw my nan putting boxes and bags into her yellow convertible. When I asked her what she was doing, she didn't really answer. Then, she gave me a gentle hug and said, 'You be a good girl for your mum and dad.'

'Nan, where are you going?'

But she still wouldn't answer and I stood open-mouthed as my nan got in her car and drove away.

Nan had moved out. Just like that.

I have absolutely no idea what had happened or why she left that Saturday morning. I do remember running desperately up to her bedroom, throwing open the door and finding all her things were gone. Where Nan had lived in our house, there now lay an empty room.

CHAPTER 3: *Struggling*

After Nan's sudden departure, life for our little family seemed to get more and more chaotic as my parents struggled to manage. The electricity would go off from time to time, when we ran out of money for the meter, plunging the house into darkness. The gas was cut off periodically as bills were not always paid. I remember peering out of the living-room window to spot the gas man, then as he came up the overgrown path, Mum whispering ferociously in my ear, 'Don't let him in, don't let him in.' But eventually he did get in.

Nan would visit every Saturday and bring cakes from the bakery. Sometimes she would take me out to the shops and we'd go to Marks & Spencer, just to look around, or sometimes buy some food. Then we'd go back to her new flat, which she'd rented in a smarter part of Cheltenham. It was in a red-bricked Victorian house fringed by tall, dark trees and was owned by an old lady who lived downstairs in the garden flat, with loads of lodgers upstairs. Nan's flat was very warm and cosy – I loved going there. She had a brownish-beige chintz sofa with a wooden frame and I would lie on it, like Princess Aurora, watching TV. If I stayed with her overnight, I would sleep on the sofa and she'd bring me a cup of tea before bedtime, then she'd tuck me up. She's still got that sofa. It's not so smart now, but it reminds me of a time when I felt snuggled up and safe.

Life certainly changed for the better when I was about four and a half and started to go to the local school, which was about a fifteen-minute walk from our house. Dad would take me to school and I'd walk beside him, holding his hand, dressed in my little green, grey and white school uniform and a pair of shoes my nan had bought especially for school – they were black patent with little diamanté butterflies on them. I guess my parents must have got the uniform secondhand through the school somehow.

Each classroom had a different pet and I loved to help look after them. I liked my teacher, too, who was very kind to me. She would let me play with Lego as much as I wanted – I was really quite obsessed with it. The other thing I loved about school was the books. I would pore over their pages endlessly in the book corner, taking in the pictures and beginning to make out the words. We were taught the *Letterland* alphabet, which was like a wonderland to me, spurring my imagination as I thought about all the characters that went with the letters.

However, although I was now surrounded by children of my own age, I didn't find it that easy to make friends at school. I think I was just not used to socializing with other children and I didn't really know what you had to do to become friends. In the end I gravitated towards shy loners. During this first year of school I remember being invited to my first (and probably only) birthday party, for a pretty girl called Melanie. I didn't really know what to do at the party and just sat in a corner watching. I couldn't take my eyes off the table, which was almost groaning with the weight of the most amazing array of food. At the end of the party I was given a goodie bag, which I clasped in my tight little fist all the way home. Once in the house, I rushed upstairs to my bedroom, closed the door and gingerly opened the bag. There was a big slice of birthday cake and I remember stuffing it down as fast as I could. It was like finding a hoard of buried treasure in a pirate's chest. Cake. All for me. Yummy.

Then my dad forgot to pick me up from school one day. It happened once, then again, then became a regular occurrence and I'd have to wait for ages until he eventually arrived. I didn't mind that much – it meant I could carry on playing with Lego and reading books.

Because my parents had to go to the drug clinic at the hospital every day, they had to rush to get me out of the house and off to school before their appointment. By the time I was around five years old I think it was getting harder and harder for them to function properly and sometimes, when they couldn't get me ready in time, I would miss school altogether.

The teachers were starting to worry that now not only was my dad not always picking me up on time, but that I was also missing whole days of school and was beginning to fall behind. I guess they, or the Head, must have reported this to the education authority and social services.

To make things worse, when I was about six my mum fell ill with a bout of meningitis. My father and nan were really struggling to look after my mum and myself and were not getting any help; they were desperately worried about what was going to happen to us all. Then Nan had a chance encounter, an innocent conversation that was to have terrible consequences for her beloved grandchild.

Nan was shopping in Cheltenham when she bumped into Eunice Spry's daughter, Judith. They remembered each other from way back, when Eunice had taken care of me for a month. They started to chat and Nan asked Judith if Eunice was still fostering children. When Judith said she was, my nan felt as if a weight had been lifted from her shoulders, suddenly hopeful that there might be a way out of what had seemed an impossible situation. She asked if Judith could ask her mother to help my parents, who were sinking fast.

Nan only wanted to help her family out at a difficult time. Eunice had looked after me well before and proved she was trustworthy. Why should Nan think that anything had changed? She was not to know what would be unleashed by bringing Eunice back into our lives.

A few days later the doorbell rang. We didn't have a phone at the time – only an old-fashioned handset in the living room with a dial that didn't work – so we couldn't have had any warning. I remember coming downstairs and climbing over the green sofa in the hall to peek at who my father was talking to through an open living-room window. I could just see someone, beyond his head, and the glint of the street light on glasses. As they talked I could see the steam rising from their breath, as it was deep in the winter, just before the new year of 1991.

Finally, Dad stepped back and signalled to the visitor to go round to the back of the house. From out of the gloom of the kitchen stepped a woman who seemed warm and friendly, dressed in a sensible red anorak and matching trousers. She was ushered into the living room, where she picked her way through the mess to sit down with my parents. I hovered in the doorway, filled with curiosity, unsure as to what I should do.

Then the woman summoned me over, delved into her huge handbag and brought out three balls of pale blue wool and some plastic knitting needles. She pulled me onto her lap and, holding my hands with the needles in them, began to show me how to knit, which fascinated me. It was lovely having someone unexpectedly bring me a present, and take the time to show me how to do something.

The woman chatted with my parents in a friendly, lively way, then asked if we would all like to go over to her house for a meal soon. A meal? At her house? Apart from going to Nan's, we never visited other people so that sounded amazing to me. Shyly, I said that yes, we would like that very much.

The woman stood up, leaving me with the knitting needles and wool, and it was agreed that we would go over to her place the following weekend for dinner. Sunday dinner! As she left, and the back door closed behind her, I turned to my parents and asked who the kind lady was.

It was none other than Eunice Spry.

CHAPTER 4: *George Dowty Drive*

Looking back now I can see how I must have seemed like the sweetest little ripe cherry, ready for the picking. With her gimlet eyes, which missed nothing, Eunice must have entered our house and seen the disorder that pointed unmistakably to a family in trouble.

The next Sunday Eunice duly came to fetch us in her large mustard Volvo estate car and drove my mother and me over to her detached house at 24 George Dowty Drive in Northway, Tewkesbury. My father stayed at home; I don't know why he didn't come. At that point I don't think I even knew that I had spent a month with Eunice when I was just a year and a half. I was only to understand this later, when my case was being prepared and we tried to work out how Eunice had come to have our family firmly within her over-controlling, greedy grasp.

But Eunice had obviously had a connection with me from my early life as she even had a photo of me as a sweet little baby. At that point nobody had any evidence to suggest that Eunice would be anything but good for our family.

She was a registered childminder, looking after children aged between a few weeks and a few months. She had already adopted Charlotte and Sarah, so the idea of her befriending our family again, with a possible view to fostering, seemed the perfect solution.

Eunice's home was an ex-council house, which she had bought on a government right-to-buy scheme. It was part of a modern housing estate in Northway on the rural outskirts of Tewkesbury and was situated in a cul-de-sac that looked a bit like Brookside Close, with neat sixties-style houses in the middle of fields and a primary school near by. There was a Co-op, a pub and a post office within walking distance, although the place had a fairly isolated, rural feel about it and was certainly different from the busy Cheltenham suburb I'd been used to.

My first impression of her house was 'wow'. It seemed warm and cosy and it looked clean, at first glance anyway. Above all, it was full of toys: exciting things like Barbie dolls and Lego. I went into the living room, which was on the right of the hall from the front door. It was originally one long room but now it had a false wall, covered with rainforest paper, right down the middle of it. When I peeked through a small door cut into the wall I was utterly amazed: there was a whole room full of toys of all sorts, shapes and sizes. It was like a toy shop in there, and all I could think was, W*ow, wow, wow, I want to stay here and play.*

The other amazing thing was that there was a Letterland border all the way round the top of the room, like a frieze. I thought this was the coolest thing ever. The woman obviously liked children and had their best interests at heart.

But best of all were Eunice's cats. Big, furry, beautiful cats. Not just a couple, but five, all with amazing names. Eunice introduced me to Tommy, an old black and white, stiff with arthritis and blind; then there was Tiger, a real moggy, silver mackerel in colour with a white chest; then, Poppy, who was similar to Tiger, Greypaws, who was, well, grey all over and Bobo, again like Tiger, only brown.

I was in heaven, not only fascinated by the family of cats but also by the lovebirds and a mini parrot in a cage in Eunice's long garden. I stared at the colourful birds, amazed that anyone could keep them as pets in their back garden.

During that first visit I met the two adopted girls who were living with Eunice already. Charlotte was about eighteen months older than me and had been with her since birth. Eunice was very affectionate towards Charlotte, who seemed like a real mummy's girl. She was a chunky child, with freckles and narrow eyes. Her ears stuck out through her mousey hair. I didn't particularly take to her and could see straight away that she was quite bossy. Eunice said to her, 'Charlotte, this is Alloma. Can you be nice to her and show her your toys?' Charlotte didn't look very friendly, but took me through the little door into the play area and showed me her dolls.

After I'd looked at the toys with Charlotte, I saw Sarah. She was six months younger than me and very skinny, with lank dark hair. She hovered timidly at the top of the stairs, looking very uncertain of herself and asked me in a small voice if I would like to go up and see her room. I thought it strange that she didn't come down and when I didn't go up straight away she went back into her room and didn't come out again. Eunice never called her down or spoke to her. I saw Eunice being a mum to Charlotte that evening, but not to Sarah, who just hid in the background, keeping out of the way.

When dinner was served that first Sunday we sat round the table like a proper family. Eunice had made a nut roast, which, looking back, was an odd choice. I had envisaged a big joint of meat, but, no, it was nuts. It was all bitty and pulpy and I didn't like it much, but there were roasted vegetables, gravy and a pudding. Sarah was still hiding in her room and I did wonder briefly why Eunice didn't go and fetch her. But I was hungry and there was loads of food, so we all tucked in together and I forgot about the little girl left upstairs on her own. It felt good – actually really exciting – to sit at a big, round table, eating a meal in a civilized way, with my mother, Charlotte and Eunice, the grown-ups chatting away.

After dinner, we were allowed to play for a while with the toys and watch a video. Eunice even did some washing in her machine for my mum. Then after that I had a hot bath with the girls. I did feel a bit shy as I didn't know the other girls at all, but it did seem quite a natural thing to do, if a little embarrassing. Then we were dressed in clean pyjamas and just as I was saying goodbye to the cats, feeling warm and clean with a nice full tummy, Eunice asked me if I'd like to come again. I blurted out 'Yes' before I could even think about it. Of course I would, what with the toys, the food and the cats. It would be wonderful.

After that first visit we were invited over to Eunice's house a couple more times for dinner. The visits ran along similar lines to the first one, in that I'd get to play with the toys and the cats, we'd have dinner at the table and a hot bath, and then I'd be taken home, well fed and wearing clean pyjamas. I was about six and a half when the visits became a bit more regular. Then I was asked if I'd like to stay the night. Just me. I felt very privileged.

I was sitting cross-legged on the carpet, stroking Tommy the cat, who was stretched out beside me, purring loudly, when Eunice came in and stood next to me. I guess she'd been watching me for a moment or two, but I had been totally engrossed in Tommy as I loved the feel of his fur running through my little fingers.

'You like Tommy?' said Eunice suddenly.

I looked up and nodded.

'He can be your special cat when you come and visit, if you like.'

I suddenly realized she was watching me intently.

'I'll get some cat biscuits so you can feed him, too. Would you like that?'

Would I like that? 'Yes, yes, I would,' I said, nodding vigorously and smiling. I couldn't believe I would have my own animal to feed and look after.

'Good then, that's settled.'

Eunice turned and strode across the room, while I went back to stroking Tommy. My very own cat. This was something I'd dreamed about.

During another visit, I was devotedly feeding Tommy with the cat biscuits Eunice had bought me when she came over and watched me carefully for a moment before saying, 'Charlotte and Sarah don't go to school like you, you know? I teach them here, at home.'

I stopped feeding Tommy and looked up at her. Eunice bent over and stroked the cat while I picked up another cat biscuit and fed it to him.

'Would you like that, too?'

I paused from tending Tommy and thought about it for a moment. I loved school. I liked the toys, the writing, the teachers, the school dinners. It was good to get away from the house, and run outside in the playground, too. But when I looked around at the Letterland border and all those toys in the special little playroom it was tempting. Suddenly, the idea of being taught here, with lessons round the dining-room table, toys and videos to play with, hot baths and food to eat, seemed very cosy indeed. It began to sound like a good idea and Charlotte and Sarah appeared to like it.

'I dunno,' I said. 'Maybe.'

'Well, you think about it,' said Eunice brightly, 'you might like it well enough.'

I did start thinking about it and even began to feel a bit jealous of both Charlotte and Sarah. School wasn't as interesting now as it used to be when compared to the excitement of being at Eunice's house all day.

At this time, I loved to watch the Letterland video at Eunice's and copy down the letters carefully in my spidery, childish hand. One day at the dining-room table I made up a 'Clever Cat' Café (Clever Cat being 'C'), drawing pictures and cutting things out to stick on cardboard, all of which I loved doing. I got a gold star sticker afterwards from Eunice – the first I'd ever got for anything at all, so it meant the world to me. Plus, I got to watch a video as a reward, something I'd never get to do at home: after all, we had no video and the TV was largely off-limits.

Over a period of about a year, from when I was six and a half to seven and a half, I'd visit Eunice more regularly. Over that time, I obviously got to know the two adopted girls better, as well as Eunice's daughter Judith. I even met her first ex-husband, father of her own children. Eunice had been married and divorced for a second time by then, yet her first husband still seemed to worship her, calling her 'my pet', despite her being quite offhand with him. Later, I would come to understand that she treated him terribly and would finally succeed in driving him away, as she had already done with husband number two.

At this time, while I was being slowly initiated into her household regime as a new member of the fold, her ex was a welcome occasional presence. He would bring us bags of reduced-price cakes from Asda – crispy scones and other treats – and he even bought me a hula hoop once from Toys 'R' Us. He was devoted to his dog, so I guess he and Eunice had a shared interest in animals. Or maybe her interest in him was based purely on his usefulness, almost as if he were another one of her household pets.

After a while, a pattern to my visits emerged: I would spend the week in Cheltenham with my family, then be picked up by Eunice in her Volvo and driven over to Tewkesbury for the weekend. As well as Charlotte and Sarah there would sometimes be a boy called Thomas staying with Eunice. He was a few years younger than me.

I now know from the evidence gathered for the court case that Eunice 'groomed' my mum. She bribed her with presents, offers of washing and cooking and the promise of a good life for her daughter, so that she would entrust me to Eunice's care. In fact, it came out in court that Eunice made a private arrangement with my mum after she had been de-registered by Gloucestershire Social Services as an official foster carer as they felt she already had enough children in her care. My parents had no idea that Eunice was no longer an 'official' carer and later I would come to understand how clever and devious she was when it came to playing officials off against each other. Although she had adopted Charlotte and Sarah and therefore wouldn't be entitled to extra money for them, she would receive a substantial weekly allowance for children she fostered. I guess Eunice wanted to increase the number of children in her care, and with it her income, as much as she possibly could. So she had been working on my parents, especially my mum, who had seen that I was well cared for and happy when I stayed with her.

Then one day my parents called me into the living room. I could see they looked very worried.

'We've got something to tell you,' said my dad sombrely.

I wondered for a moment if Tommy had run away or died; I worried about him when I was away from him. I looked at Mum, who was looking very sad, lying on the sofa, and at Dad, who was clearly struggling to be brave. It must be bad, whatever it was.

'You know you like going to Eunice's for the weekend? Well—' my dad paused and looked at the floor, 'you'll be living there from now on.'

I remember feeling a bit scared. I liked going to Eunice's,

but being there all the time, well, I wasn't sure if I liked that idea.

'You like it there, don't you?' Dad said.

I thought of Tommy and the food and the other girls. 'Yes.'

'Well, it'll be like going on holiday,' said Dad, trying to smooth things over. 'You know your mum's not been very well, so it's for the best.'

Mum was clearly crying now so I crawled over to her and she put her arms around me. I felt sad and scared because I loved my mum, but I also felt a twinge of excitement if I am totally honest. As the idea settled in my mind I thought it might be fun to get away for a while, and anyway, I didn't feel as if I had any choice in the matter, so I had to go along with it.

'It's all right, Mum, I'll be fine.'

'Yeah, love, I'm sure you will,' said Mum, through her tears.

I had no reason to think at that point that it wouldn't be the best thing in the world: Mum needed a break because she was ill again. Anyway, I thought, it wouldn't be for long.

CHAPTER 5: *Brainwashed*

So by the time I was seven and a half I had begun to live full-time at 24 George Dowty Drive and the pattern of my life had completely reversed. I would visit my parents for an occasional weekend or evening, and Eunice's house was now to be called 'home'.

Moving to Eunice's full-time meant I had to change schools. I hadn't made a best friend in my old school, so it wasn't really a big wrench. By sheer coincidence it was another bottle green, grey and white uniform. When I went to the new school they put me in Reception, I think because I was quite small, but also because I was probably quite behind educationally having missed a lot of school. However, I soon caught up and was even top of the class, so they moved me up a year. There were loads of toys in the classroom and I met some nice children. However, I still didn't really make friends easily; I don't think I knew how to. Plus, part of me was hankering after being taught at home, like Charlotte and Sarah were, as Eunice had made it sound so much more exciting than going to an ordinary school like everyone else.

I would now be taken to school by Eunice's daughter Judith, who was about twenty-eight at this time, with a very masculine-looking face, dark hair and eyebrows and a bit of a moustache. She was tall and strong and wore mostly baggy T-shirts and jeans. She worked in a joinery as a secretary and would drop me off at school before cycling on to work. I'd hold on to her bike's handlebars and trot alongside her while she cycled far too fast for my short legs. I'd get out of breath and would struggle to keep up. We must have looked bizarre. She was often brusque and would snap at me to 'Hurry up', which I didn't like.

Judith didn't have a boyfriend and was still living at home, which I now think was rather odd at her age. I think Judith was pretty much brainwashed by Eunice and made to feel she could not leave home and be an independent woman. With hindsight, I think Judith was having some kind of affair but it was all very furtive and I don't think Eunice ever knew about it. Anyway, Judith's role at home soon became clear to me – she was there to help keep the children in line.

When I first began living in Tewkesbury, going to a new school and getting used to new people, I think I simply accepted the situation. That was how life was. I was seven and a half, going on eight and I was quite a character by then – very chatty and curious about things, and not frightened to ask questions. One day Eunice told me, categorically, that I wouldn't live beyond ten years of age. I don't know why she told me this, but I believed it. Most children do believe what adults tell them, and to me, a seven-and-a-half-year-old, the age of ten seemed a long way off and so I thought defiantly: *I don't care.*

Not long after I arrived Thomas came to stay with us full-time. Then it was suddenly announced by Eunice that a new baby was going to come and live with us too. Again, I didn't really question who he was, and it didn't feel that strange, although now, being a mother myself, it seems quite odd. Eunice seemed to want to have loads of children around, so I just accepted it.

I remember visiting the baby in hospital. He looked very delicate, very tiny and weak. He had lots of tubes going into his little body and a bigger one up his nose, which I remember looked a bit scary. I know now that he was methadone-addicted at birth, poor little thing, and he was underweight. I remember singing to him in my squeaky voice, kissing his cheek and smelling him – that lovely smell of newborn babies, that warm, milky, cosy smell. He was in hospital for a few months as he needed to get stronger before Eunice could take him home.

By the time I was eight I was used to being at Eunice's, but I missed my parents a lot. I would tell Eunice I was missing them and she would say, 'You'll be visiting them soon,' but the promised visit would never materialize. Now I realize that from the minute I got there Eunice wanted me to forget about having had any past life and to adopt a new one in her Tewkesbury fiefdom.

The first step was to break down Thomas's and my identity, so that we lost all touch with ourselves and our heritage, just as she had done with Sarah and Charlotte. After we'd been living a while at George Dowty full-time Eunice made it clear that we were to think of her as our real parent: 'Call me Mummy,' she insisted, and as everyone else there did, we did too. However, she stressed that on the rare occasions when I was at my birth parents' house I had to remember to call her 'Auntie Eunice'.

The second thing we had to do was change our names. Eunice didn't like my name, Alloma, because it was a 'magic' name in her eyes and therefore 'demonized'. One day Thomas and I were at the table with Charlotte and Sarah when Eunice gave a book to Charlotte and said mockingly, 'Pass this to the Devil's child next to you'.

This was me. I blushed and felt very embarrassed. I looked up and Eunice showed no emotion at all. Charlotte smirked and looked at Eunice, who said maliciously, 'Yes, they're the Devil's kids all right.' Meaning both Thomas and me.

Thomas looked annoyed, but said nothing, just squirmed in his seat. Then Eunice put a piece of paper in front of me.

'There's a better choice of names for you,' she said. 'Better than your demonized name, anyway.'

I looked down and saw four names: Rebecca, Harriet, Wilhelmina and Jemima.

'You can choose one of those. Better than that evil name you've got.'

I sat and tears stung my eyes. My mother had chosen the name Alloma. It was a link with my family. But I looked up at Eunice's mean mask of a face and I knew I had to choose. No question.

There was a little girl at my school called Harriet and I quite liked the name, so I became Harriet Gilbert and dropped Alloma altogether. It felt very weird at first, but oddly, I got used to it fairly quickly. I was having to get used to a lot of new, weird things. Thus, from the age of seven I was known as Harriet and when a school friend asked me why I'd changed my name, I just said it was because I liked it. I knew better than to say, 'My foster mum thinks my real name is demonized.'

Thomas had to change his name too but because all these different names are confusing, I'm going to keep calling him Thomas!

I don't think Eunice told my parents, and anyway, I rarely saw them now. If I did, I had to pretend I was still Alloma, just as Eunice was 'Auntie Eunice'. The final touch was when Eunice insisted I drop the Gilbert part and adopt her current surname, Spry, as well. So I was forced to give up on my parents, my nan, my heritage and everything to do with my past family and home. I didn't like it much, but even at this early stage in our life together I knew better than to question Eunice. I believe that in her mind I now belonged to her, as did the other children.

I also think she hated the fact I had Romany heritage and that this contributed to her believing I was the 'Devil's child'.

One day she was combing my hair very hard and pulling it aggressively into a rubber band. It hurt like hell. I had always loved my long, dark and curly hair, particularly because it was like my mum's and reminded me of her.

'You've got gypo hair,' she said rudely.

I looked in the mirror and instantly saw myself as ugly. I saw myself through Eunice's eyes, and tears began to well up, but I blinked them back. I was not going to show weakness.

'We'll soon get rid of all this,' she said as she wrenched my hair up and into a tight ponytail. Eunice had always hated my hair and although my mother had asked her to keep it long she could not wait to chop it off.

I would look in the mirror on my own and peer at my face, running my fingers through my hair, and tears would drip down my cheeks. Was I bedevilled? Was I really evil? Eunice made me feel ugly, hideous and worth absolutely nothing.

At first my parents would write me a letter every week and Eunice would stand over me as I read them. Sometimes she would intercept the mail and keep letters from me and when I would ask, 'Has there been a letter from my mum and dad?' she would shake her head. But I couldn't believe that they had stopped writing. I would go and look at the floor below the letterbox, but if Eunice saw me looking, she would turn nasty. I was beginning to see a new, bad-tempered side of her which was very scary and which I didn't like at all.

One morning I was watching out for the post when Eunice appeared at my side, furious. 'It's no good you looking, there's nothing there,' she said roughly.

Her eyes glinted and I felt afraid and bewildered. Why was she being so odd about me getting letters from home?

'Isn't there any post today?'

'No. Now get away from the door.'

I felt I couldn't argue as her behaviour was quite terrifying. Then, soon after that morning, the letters from my parents stopped coming altogether.

I was very confused as initially I had felt that Eunice's house was a nice place to be. But she was changing and she seemed to be getting tougher towards Thomas and me in particular. I noticed, increasingly, how nice she was to Charlotte, and how harsh she was to Sarah. For instance, Charlotte had a nice room, but Sarah's room was very cold and untidy. Thomas and I had been put in to share with Sarah and when the new baby boy, Robert, arrived he was allowed to stay with Eunice. It was like there was a ranking order, with Charlotte and

Robert at the top, and Sarah, Thomas and me at the bottom. We had to 'serve' the other two quite often, making sure they had their food first, had the best toys or watched the videos they wanted. We were made to feel we were second best all the time, which was hurtful and humiliating.

When we'd been there for about six months to a year, Eunice stepped up her campaign to warp my mind against my parents and really began to brainwash me – all of us, in fact – about the nature of my parents.

One day, we were in the kitchen clearing up the dishes after a meal when Eunice suddenly blurted out, 'Of course, your parents are big drug addicts, they're hopeless people. You do know that, don't you?'

Eunice was glaring at me, but I was shocked and outraged, so I leapt to their defence. This was my mum and dad she was talking about. How dare she?

'No, they're not, they're nice.'

Eunice continued to stare at me fiercely through her big glasses for a moment, her lips compressed together in a thin line – a look I was learning to dread; it was really scary.

'It's time you knew the truth – your mum's had loads of abortions. Do you know what that means? She kills babies.'

I was shocked at the idea of my mum killing a baby, and while I know now that this was untrue, at the time it confused me because I did have a very early memory of my mum telling me about a stillborn baby – I think it was a girl – when I was really little. But Eunice insisted my mother had aborted the baby, which sounded terrible and upset me hugely. She made it sound as though my mum had killed her with her own bare hands. The stillbirth was something that I had talked about a lot when I was little. I used to tell children at my two different schools that I'd had a sister who had died. But the idea that my mum had killed her, on purpose, well, that was horrible, unthinkable.

On another occasion, Eunice was preparing dinner, chopping onions, while I sat drawing at the table, when she launched into her now familiar mantra: 'Of course, you know your parents are hopeless drug addicts. They're totally possessed by the Devil. They're evil.'

I looked up at her, furious. I was very loyal to my parents and quite feisty.

'You can't say that. You can't!' I blurted out.

Eunice turned around, knife in hand, and fixed me with an icy glare. I felt the blood draining away from my face. My mouth opened, but the more she stared, the less I was able to speak.

'You were saying?'

I opened my mouth, but again no sound came out. All I could see were her steely eyes boring fiercely into me. My eyes moved from hers to the knife and back. I closed my mouth. I felt defeated, even though I knew in my heart of hearts that what she was saying was wrong.

On my eighth birthday I was lucky enough to see my parents alone. It was the only time I'd seen them without Eunice as a chaperone since going to live with her. Dad bought me a little gold-coloured locket that day in a toy shop in the shopping arcade in Cheltenham, which I thought was truly beautiful. It was a gold, heart-shaped frame with a white and pink porcelain rose picture in it. I treasured this present and carried it everywhere until it eventually disappeared when I was about thirteen.

After I'd seen my parents on my birthday Eunice bought a Barbie doll for me from a big shop in Cheltenham, seemingly determined to outdo my parents or to eradicate the good feeling I had about my dad's present. These gifts might well have been some sort of bribe to make me think fondly of her, or perhaps she feared she might lose me to my parents as a result of our having spent time together unchaperoned.

Sometimes the phone would go in Eunice's living room and I would hear my parents leaving messages. One time I picked up the phone and was speaking to my dad when suddenly Eunice snatched the handset roughly out of my hand and hung up. Just like that. She didn't explain, but the way she did it told me enough to know I was not to pick up the phone again. I was shocked, but I didn't say anything. Or try to ring back. I guess I just felt that I couldn't, especially when she looked that fearsome.

Another time I blurted out at the dinner table that I'd seen my parents having sex one night back home. I had heard my mum calling out my dad's name loudly over and over and had thought, at first, that he was hurting her, so I got up, and then I saw they were doing something odd-looking together in the dark. Just as I said this, Eunice leapt up and clamped her large hand over my mouth, her grey eyes staring at me wildly, her face only a few inches from mine. I learned from this that sex was something not to be spoken about, particularly over a meal. Even though, or maybe especially, if what I said was true.

Thus, the age of eight became a milestone for me because it was at this age that Eunice actually succeeded in cutting me off from my parents.

Another significant event that sticks out in my mind from that early time at George Dowty is one which made me realize pretty quickly how differently Thomas and I would be treated from the new baby, Robert. For two weeks Eunice shut Thomas and me up in a tiny bedroom and wouldn't let us out. She didn't lock the door, but made it clear that we were not free to roam around the house or garden. The reason? We had colds and were not allowed out in case the baby got infected. It made no sense to us but showed what Eunice really thought about us in relation to Robert.

While we were shut in Eunice told us to do a strange thing, which we did obediently, of course, no questions asked: we were to count up to a hundred in our heads and then blow our noses. Over and over and over again. So we would spend all day, shut in this tiny bedroom, counting up to a hundred and blowing our noses, then counting up to a hundred again, and blowing again. When Eunice wasn't around or within earshot, we'd relax and play with each other for a bit. But the minute we heard her foot on the stair or her voice on the landing, we'd start counting to a hundred, then nose blowing again. Indeed, this bizarre ritual went on for two whole weeks, an eternity for two small children. I have no idea why Eunice made us do this, but I'm sure that most of what she did was about control, trying to out-psych us, all the time.

One afternoon after this strange confinement, I went swimming with Charlotte, having some much-needed fun. By chance we met two of Charlotte's estranged biological siblings at the swimming pool. We came bounding into the house together afterwards and I blurted out, 'Oooh, we've just seen Charlotte's brother and sister at the pool.' Eunice looked up quickly from the kitchen sink, turned and then strode towards me, a terrifying look on her face. She seemed to have grown in size and was towering over me, her face white and taut with barely suppressed rage.

'Oh, no you didn't, they were *just friends*.'

Charlotte said nothing and looked down. She obviously knew not to quibble. But being headstrong back then, I opened my mouth. I didn't know any better.

'*But we did*, we saw her brother and sister. We were in the shower together after swimming, at the pool.'

Eunice suddenly leant forwards and tapped me on the mouth quite sharply. I was taken aback, as it hurt; I thought, *Why is she doing that? What have I done wrong?* I couldn't understand what the problem was, yet I also felt warned off, that I shouldn't say anything more about the incident. I wasn't sure why, but I knew I was stepping into dangerous territory. I was learning quickly that there were many things I had to keep quiet about.

Satisfied with having put down any whiff of rebellion, Eunice calmly went back to the sink and resumed her chores.

With hindsight I can see how Eunice had begun her mission to control everything that we did, thought and believed. That first sharp tap on the mouth to silence me was merely the mildest taster of what was to come.

CHAPTER 6: *A New Religion*

As Eunice began to mistreat Sarah, Thomas and me on a more regular basis, starting with flicks and hits on the mouth and then clouts to the head, my parents, totally unaware of what was happening at George Dowty, moved into a flat in the same large Victorian house that my nan had gone to live in when she left us, way back, when I was about four. I only saw my parents a couple of times again and when I did, I knew better than to let on that anything was amiss for fear of being severely punished by Eunice. By then it had been driven into me that I had to be perfectly behaved and demure when I went out of the house, especially because Eunice went with us everywhere and would be watching every twitch and listening to every word, so that there would be hell to pay later if I put a foot out of line.

Eunice's mindset and the evangelical language she used, her talk of the Devil and demons, were influenced by her own strange interpretation of the Jehovah's Witness faith. Her faith was a big part of her life and soon became part of mine too because it wasn't long after Thomas and I went to live with her that she started taking us to Jehovah's Witness meetings. I already believed in Jesus, having been taught about him at my first school. As a little girl I really believed that I loved Jesus. This, however, was not enough for Eunice, who wanted all us children to share her own beliefs. Thomas and I were new to the religion and she would tell us we came from Satanists; we had to go with her to her religious meetings to try to save our evil souls.

Eunice went to Jehovah's Witness meetings in Tewkesbury three or four times a week, taking us all with her. There was a Sunday meeting at the Kingdom Hall, when we would listen to a talk from an elder and have a *Watchtower* study. There were three other meetings during the week: one where the adults would be trained how to go door to door to teach about the religion; on Tuesdays Eunice would go round to a couple's house where there were little groups studying religious books together; and on Thursdays she would go to the Kingdom Hall and listen to talks about public speaking.

At the meetings we children were always told to sit quietly and be well behaved while the adults studied their books and we pretended to study ours. I read in one book that Jesus wasn't crucified, as I'd been told at school, but that he'd died on an upright pole, which I found both confusing and upsetting.

I would sometimes be given a picture book of Bible stories,

although I could read quite well by then, but at least the pictures would entertain me for a while. However, I did eventually find the meetings quite boring, and I didn't like it when I had to read a paragraph of a study book and then talk about it in front of everyone. This was called 'Answers Up'. I really dreaded 'answering up' as it made me very self-conscious, especially with Eunice's eagle eye trained on me all the time, waiting for me to make a mistake for which she could punish me later at home.

The Jehovah's Witnesses taught us that Jesus was not to be worshipped or prayed to because he is God's son but not equal to God, and was resurrected in spirit only. They don't believe in hell, or that people have an immortal soul that goes to heaven when they die. But people can be resurrected by God. They talked a lot about the fact that we were in the End Times, that Armageddon was coming and when it did only 144,000 anointed would go to heaven. The rest of the Jehovah's Witnesses (and other people as well) would live in paradise on earth.

The celebration of festive days, like Christmas, Easter, even birthdays, was forbidden because of their pagan origins. They taught us that as much as possible we should mix only with Jehovah's Witnesses, keeping our 'outside contact' with other people to a minimum. All Jehovah's Witnesses were to be called 'brother' or 'sister' even though they weren't our real family.

Eunice's bizarre twist on her religion gave her a plausible excuse for her constant abuse of us children. She explained, painstakingly, that discipline was part of religion. I think discipline *was* Eunice's religion, in and for itself. Eunice said that I had to behave, I had to be honest and not lie or I would die. Her explanation of anything about the Jehovah's Witnesses was always very dramatic and full of gore and nasty stuff. It wasn't just that I would die, but that I would die in a really horrible, slow and painful way. She was all fire and brimstone and it made my flesh creep. Scared children would be obedient children: I guess that was the general idea.

She would tell us that we would die if we did not obey and fear God. But, she added, we would also die if we just obeyed God out of fear. So, she said we'd die anyway because we were scared and didn't love God – it was all very confusing.

Eunice used to terrify us with stories of what would happen at Armageddon, when the soldiers came to get us and put us to the sword. Our eyes would melt, our skin would burn, and we would feel the most terrible, excruciating pain we could possibly imagine. I used to have nightmares thinking about it, and hated looking at the pictures of Armageddon in the magazines. Eunice made us watch horror films so that we would understand what Armageddon and hell would be like. The films were not age appropriate and were very upsetting, even traumatizing.

Thomas and I would often fight with each other terribly and

on one occasion, when I bit him, Eunice told me he would die from the germs that I'd infected him with. She made me think I was diseased and that this one bite might kill him. For years I believed this, feeling bad about myself and guilty about him. The idea that blood carries not only bad character traits but also germs was central to Eunice's whole mindset. She truly believed that I was the Devil's child, rotten and evil through and through, because of my heritage, which she drummed into my brain over and over and over again. Therefore, my blood was dirty, evil, contaminated.

Eunice's own parents, Katie and John, were also devout Jehovah's Witnesses and she'd grown up in the faith. However, given that extramarital and premarital sex was forbidden, I did find something strange in a drawer in Eunice's house once: a picture of her wearing skimpy underwear, with two men on a bed, obviously engaged in some type of sexual activity, doing a V-sign at the camera. I never asked her about it, as I couldn't ask her about anything, and, anyway, I could hardly own up to having poked about in a drawer, or to having found such a picture. I certainly would have been punished. Nevertheless, it registered in my mind as being extremely out of character. Or was it? I later found out that she had been thrown out of the Jehovah's Witnesses at one time – 'disfellowshipped' as they call it – for something or other, but that she had somehow wormed her way back in. Eunice could be very persuasive, very seductive. She had, after all, managed to seduce two husbands successfully before I met her.

Grandiosely, Eunice would tell me that she was the best Jehovah's Witness around, the most devoted follower, as she did not spare the rod with children. She was often quite disparaging about the other Jehovah's Witnesses we came into contact with, telling us they weren't true believers, because they were too soft. Indeed, I would later find out that there were very good Jehovah's Witnesses around, who didn't advocate beating and abusing children. They believed in being firm, but not horribly violent and ritualistic, like Eunice was. But I would learn that only much later, once the damage was done. Ironically, I would ultimately be grateful to those Jehovah's Witnesses that Eunice thought were 'soft'.

I'm still trying to understand whether Eunice's behaviour was born of a religious belief that she needed to 'teach us a lesson' or whether she sincerely felt that what she made us do, or what she did to us, was 'improving' to our characters, our health and was saving our evil souls. Either way, her outlook was punitive and extreme, with everything divided into black and white, good and evil. With Eunice as the judge. Most of the time we were in a no-win situation: if we owned up to a 'Sin', we'd get punished, but if we didn't own up (also a Sin), we'd also get punished. We were damned if we did, and damned if we didn't.

CHAPTER 7: *Taming the Devil's Child*

When I look back on living with Eunice's regime I think of it as going down a flight of steps to a basement. On the first few steps, I had to get acclimatized to the drop in light and temperature. As I went on, it began to feel damp and uncomfortable, until finally, I descended into a cold, rat-infested, stinking cellar where I was tortured sadistically until I screamed for mercy. But no mercy came.

The first eighteen months in Eunice's house gave me an idea of what life with her would be like: full of rules, bizarre rituals, a weird and idiosyncratic routine, with endless things we had to remember on pain of punishment.

Every morning we were subjected to a ritual toilet check. We were made to eat All-Bran with a couple of tablespoons of linseeds sprinkled on top. I didn't like it particularly, but as we were told, 'You'll eat what you're given,' there was no choice. There was no fruit or toast or other cereal and you simply couldn't refuse. We were meant to feel grateful that we were getting food at all, given what we'd come from.

Eunice was particularly hard on Sarah. Every morning she would make Sarah go to the toilet and then follow her there to inspect what she had done. She would examine the toilet's contents sternly through her glasses and Sarah would have to say to Eunice, 'Mummy, I've done my poo,' and be very obedient and demure about it.

One of the problems with having to poo to order every morning is that you can't always do it – our bodies just don't work that way. Still Eunice would make us sit there, straining away, and we couldn't come off until we'd delivered. It was the rule. It was terrible and I was petrified. But the more anxious I got, the less I was able to poo, of course. And not only did I have to poo before I went to school, I was also forbidden to do one at any other time of day. If I did, I had to hide it.

I remember the panic I felt when Eunice started checking on me because I'd seen Sarah sent to her room as a punishment for not measuring up. Sarah was very withdrawn all the time, but especially during these morning checks. Everybody thought she was autistic but I think she was just utterly terrified – too afraid to speak, to show any feelings, even to move or breathe.

But the punishment didn't end there. If we didn't come up with the goods in the morning Eunice would administer an enema. The big syringe would come out filled with green washing-up liquid mixed with water to make it frothy. I would look at the huge pointed end of the syringe and the solution sloshing around and think, *No way is that going inside me.* But, as with everything in Eunice's regime, it was impossible to escape. She would bark at me to pull my pants down and bend over and I would have to comply. Eunice would then shove the syringe up my backside, not caring that it was uncomfortable, snapping, 'Relax, relax your bum muscles' as she pushed it in hard. Next she'd push the plunger in and I'd fill right up with the soapy liquid which I had to hold in for half an hour, sometimes an hour, even two hours or more, depending on her mood. It created the most enormous pressure inside my body and I wanted to get it out of me as soon as I could, but she insisted that I held it in. Then, when I eventually let it all out, it squirted everywhere, causing a stinking mess.

I would go to school feeling utterly horrible, hoping no one knew what had been done to me at home. Sometimes I'd continue to dribble and leak during the day and I'd have brown stains on my pants, which felt very humiliating.

The poo check and enema regime continued day in, day out until I finally escaped from Eunice when I was seventeen.

If Eunice thought we were lying, had spoken out of turn or said something blasphemous, we would be summoned to the kitchen sink. The first time it happened I had no idea what she was doing. She just stood there for a moment before picking up the washing-up liquid bottle.

'Stand still and open your mouth,' she ordered.

As she moved towards me, I could see she was aiming the nozzle of the bottle at my mouth and I naturally jerked away. Sensing my resistance, Eunice grabbed my long hair hard and yanked my head back. I was in her iron grip and she was only inches away. She then pushed the nozzle of the bottle into my mouth so I could taste the pine and feel the slime.

Suddenly I felt a huge squirt shoot into my mouth. I could feel it running over my tongue and teeth, heading for my throat.

'Swallow,' commanded Eunice, still holding my head back forcefully.

I swallowed the disgusting stuff and she carried on squirting. 'I'm washing your mouth out with soap because you told a lie,' she said as she continued to squeeze.

By now I was choking and I could feel the slimy soap churning horribly in my stomach. Eunice then released my head suddenly and I almost toppled over. I felt sick and disgusting; she simply went back to the sink and plonked the bottle down on the drainer.

I saw Eunice do this to the other children too, particularly Sarah and Thomas. In fact, I saw Judith take shampoo and force it down Sarah's throat in the bathroom once. Judith had learned Eunice's tricks and would use them with the same force and ferocity.

When I had washing-up liquid or shampoo squirted down my throat it was difficult not to be sick. This, however, brought with it an even more vile punishment.

One day, we were lined up at the sink, waiting to have our mouths washed out as Eunice believed we'd all lied about something. Charlotte was left out of this, but I was behind Sarah, whose turn was next. I saw Eunice yank her head back and she must have administered a particularly large dollop because Sarah threw it up, leaving a pile of half-digested All-Bran and linseeds covered with washing-up liquid in the sink.

Keeping hold of Sarah's hair, Eunice snapped, 'Eat it.'

Sarah was shaking and crying helplessly, but Eunice didn't care. We all watched as she got a spoon and lifted a mouthful of slop to Sarah's quivering lips.

'Eat it, or you'll get worse.'

Crying silently, Sarah took the spoon's contents and chewed, retching as she did so.

'Swallow.'

Eunice was relentless as spoonful by spoonful, the mess in the sink was forced into Sarah's mouth. She had to eat the lot.

I watched, horrified. I felt sick just seeing Sarah having to eat her vomit, knowing full well that I was next. How could I escape? Thomas was behind me and Charlotte watched, sniggering, from the other side of the room. There was no way I could run away from this ritual humiliation, but I vowed I wouldn't be sick, no matter how ill Eunice made me feel. It was almost as if her vile treatment made me tougher in response. I decided that when it was my turn I would blank out my mind and try to keep it all down, no matter what. Watching the other kids suffer meant I soon learned to resolve not to throw up and to this day I can't bear being sick.

So what were the terrible lies that brought on this regular, daily punishment? It might have been doing a poo when I shouldn't have (a terrible offence) which, if I lied about it, resulted in the washing-up-liquid treatment. It might be lying about watching a video we weren't allowed to see or simply touching something I shouldn't have – after all she was watching me all the time, and I wouldn't necessarily know that I had done something wrong, until I was standing by the sink and that nozzle was heading towards my face.

The washing-up-liquid routine was a regular occurrence for all of us except Charlotte and Robert. It happened so many times I lost count. In fact, it's left me with a total loathing of green or yellow washing-up liquid; even if I get just a whiff of the smell, I feel utterly sick. I now won't buy either of these types, and choose fancy, expensive ones instead, only blue or other completely different colours.

Eunice not only had her eagle eye trained on all of us, making sure we all behaved as she wanted us to every minute of every day and even night, she also made us all watch and grass on each other: vigilance was her constant watchword.

Eunice read her Jehovah's Witness *Watchtower* avidly and indeed, it was as though I was constantly being watched by her from her parental watchtower. It felt like being under the gaze of a pious Big Brother. Eunice watched us when we were indoors, then when we went out into the garden, and finally, even when we went to school, as my school's grounds backed onto her house, so she could even watch me when I went out to play at break and dinner time. I would feel her eyes on me and would look up to find her staring at me fixedly from the window. I would instantly feel I'd done something wrong.

But sometimes when I was at school and peeked up at the bedroom window, I would sometimes see Sarah there, on the top bunk bed, peering out timidly at the playground. At first, I would wonder why she wasn't downstairs at her lessons with Eunice and why she was in bed. Later, I would understand she was being punished, especially when the same thing started happening to me. Sometimes, if Sarah saw me, she'd wave limply, and I'd wave back coolly. We weren't very close and didn't like each other much, but there was an understanding between us, a sense of each knowing what the other was having to endure.

Eunice's constant vigilance meant I became vigilant too, and as she was always peering out of a window trying to see where I was in the playground, so I always felt as if I was under her gaze. Whether I was or not. One thing she was monitoring was whether I was playing the games she allowed me to play or not. Eunice had strict rules about what was acceptable. For instance, I was not allowed to play cowboys and Indians as it involved the use of guns or 'Power Rangers', which were all the rage at the time. This game was 'demonized', as were many others. If I played the wrong thing, I would be punished later at home. I used to hide behind the hedge to avoid her gaze, then I'd play something forbidden, like 'Ninja Turtles', my heart in my mouth, hoping she couldn't see through the hedge. Or that someone wouldn't tell on me, somehow.

Ironically, Eunice would drum into us that playing these 'worldly' games would make us more aggressive. She said she was punishing us to save our souls. Eventually though, when she decided we were the Devil's kids, we couldn't be saved, so it was just Eunice venting her anger, by then. If I looked up and found her looking at me, she'd say to me I wasn't 'innocent', like a normal child. I was too 'aware', and thus I was 'demonized', I had the Devil in me. She said the Devil was what made me look at her when she was looking at me. Only she didn't know how many times I had looked up when either she wasn't there or when she wasn't looking.

One day at school I had been playing Power Rangers in what I thought was a safe place behind the hedge. However, Charlotte had seen and reported me to Eunice. Charlotte was the main squealer at home but Sarah sometimes buckled under the pressure.

As I came in from school Eunice was standing there, waiting for me. She looked extremely grim and I knew instantly I was in trouble.

'What were you doing?'

I had to think quickly. *What did she mean? What had I done now?*

'Nothing.'

'You evil little liar. I saw you. You were playing a demonized game. You know you were. Own up.'

Oh Lord, she saw me. I said nothing, however.

'You know you're not allowed to play worldly games. I won't allow it.'

Eunice strode over to me and grabbed me by the throat, squeezing the life out of me. For a moment everything went white, then black, and then I was back in the room, with her eyes boring into mine, her mouth, with its foul breath, only inches away. I could smell her body odour, which was always rank, as it wafted over in her excitement.

'You are not to play the Devil's own games. D'ya hear? You're not innocent enough.'

I was choking, gasping, my two hands trying to wrench her one hand away from my throat. There was no air going in at all and I was struggling against fainting altogether.

'Relax, child. I'm teaching you a lesson. It's for your own

good. You're too aware, you've got the Devil in you, for sure.'

Out of the corner of my eye, as I struggled to breathe, I could see plump Charlotte watching, looking smug. However, Sarah was peeping through the banisters at me, looking terrified, as always.

Suddenly Eunice let me go and I fell to the floor, gasping like a fish that had just been landed. My throat hurt like hell and I gulped air in as fast as I could. My head was swimming and I still felt faint. All I'd done was play a game behind the hedge – that was innocent enough for me.

By the time I was approaching nine years of age, I was doing quite well at school. I liked my lessons and the teachers, who were kind and thoughtful – the total opposite of Eunice. I loved art, especially drawing, and I also had a go on the school piano and found I was quite musical, too. There was a nice class teacher there who cast me as an angel in the school Nativity play. That Christmas I was very excited as we rehearsed the songs and lines at school. However, when the time came, nobody came to watch me; I had kept the whole thing secret from Eunice because it was against Jehovah's Witness rules. I was a bit of a star at school, but I kept quiet about it at home, knowing that Eunice would never have approved. It hurt, none the less, that nobody ever saw me shine.

When I was almost eight and a half Robert became pretty ill. As a consequence, Eunice had to stay with him in hospital and I went to stay with an old friend of hers, 'Auntie Vera', who lived next door to her parents, giving me a brief reminder of what 'normal' life was like. Eunice's mother, Katie, and father, John, only lived a stone's throw away from our house in George Dowty, and they saw Eunice quite regularly. Actually, it was a mystery to me as to why Eunice was so awful when, in fact, her mum always seemed quite nice.

Anyway, Auntie Vera treated me like a normal child for a whole week. We went to the mini-market and did our shopping and she bought me a secondhand My Little Pony – something I'd always wanted and had gone on at my parents about to no avail. But this nice lady took me out, she gave me food, she tucked me up at night, she washed my clothes and she was kind. There were no beatings. It was an utter revelation to me to be reminded of how life could be without daily, ritualistic punishment – a total respite from the horrors and pressure of living with Eunice.

This window on to normal life highlighted just how much, in the two years since I'd first set foot in 24 George Dowty Drive, things had gone downhill. For a start, Eunice was far from the generous person she had seemed to me when we first met. The knitting wool, the lovely Sunday lunch– they were all part of the seduction plan. In actual fact, she turned out to be extremely mean, a real Scrooge. When, for instance, I needed plimsolls for PE at school, she refused to buy them, which meant I often couldn't do PE, although I was desperate to join in. But she wouldn't spend money on me.

In hindsight, I think that while Eunice was undoubtedly mean and penny-pinching, another major reason for preventing me from doing PE was because I would have to take my clothes off, and then the pupils and teachers would see my bruises. Similarly, the swimming I had once adored was stopped, which again, I now realize, was not only because of the cost but also because someone might spot the obvious signs of my maltreatment. School trips were also forbidden because they cost money and I clearly wasn't worth it. And she would have worried about me being beyond her control – who knows, I might have spilled the beans and someone might have believed me.

I remember once when, for some reason, I was supposed to go home at lunch time to eat but Eunice was out when I got there. When I went back to school and told my teacher there was no one home, she gave me a school dinner and a receipt to take back to Eunice for £1.50. Eunice went ballistic and clouted me hard around the head saying, 'Why didn't you eat the apples from the garden?' So the next time I came home for lunch and nobody was there, I knew better than to take the offer of a school meal and pleaded with my teacher, 'Please don't give me a school dinner, because I'll be in a lot of trouble.' I remember one of the teachers giving me one of his own mustard and ham sandwiches, which I ate in the staff room.

Around this time, too, what had been a nice, neat school uniform was beginning to look quite shabby. I must have looked different from other children, always wearing charity shop hand-me-downs and being unnaturally obedient. Indeed, I found out, during the court case, that several of the teachers had been worried about me and one had even written several letters to Gloucester Social Services, although I obviously didn't know about that at the time. In fact, I think Eunice did have a visit from someone, but she was able to pull the wool over their eyes, as always.

Also, the house in George Dowty, which had seemed such a cosy paradise at first, was also becoming increasingly messy. Eunice was a real hoarder, and would never throw anything away, so rooms began to fill up with junk and there were ever-growing mounds of clutter everywhere. I found this very distressing and would sometimes pick up armfuls of junk and simply plonk it all in a bin. However, in a silent war of wills, Eunice would simply take it all out again and put it back in my room or the shared rooms.

And not only was the house beginning to be messy, it was dirty, too. This is something that would simply get worse and worse over the years to come.

CHAPTER 8: *Good Books and Bad Books*

I soon learned at George Dowty Drive there were so-called 'Good Books' and 'Bad Books' which we children could end up in, depending on our behaviour and attitudes. It wasn't clear exactly what the rules were, as they were deeply embedded in Eunice's strange mind, but they were usually to do with how she perceived us. Thus, if she had been watching us, vigilantly, as usual, and we had done something she didn't like or approve of, we were in her Bad Books. Looking back on my first visit to George Dowty for Sunday dinner I realize that Sarah was clearly in Eunice's Bad Books that day; she was not allowed to come downstairs or eat with us and remained hovering timidly at the top of the stairs, almost afraid to breathe.

Being in Eunice's Bad Books meant punishment and it could take ages before you were able to get back into her Good Books. It was very arbitrary, too, and could flip in a moment from being Bad to Good and back again. I wanted to be in her Good Books to avoid punishment but, over the years,

I learned that I was in her Bad Books from the outset (being the Devil's child), so there was almost nothing I could do to clear my evil slate. If you're bad from birth, what can you do?

So what sort of crime would put me in her Bad Books? And what punishment would be meted out? And how could I get back into her Good Books?

I often found it hard just to drop off to sleep at night, as my mind was quite active. You have to remember I was still a small child and back home, as I mentioned earlier, I would often get out of bed and scoot around the room, just to wind down so I could get to sleep. I also sometimes had nightmares and needed some sort of comfort to settle down.

Eunice, however, expected me to go upstairs and straight to sleep. Just like that. If I didn't go to sleep, I was in her Bad Books. We girls had been given one nightie each, an old-fashioned one, made of winceyette, fleecy material. Mine was pink with long sleeves and puffy shoulders, and it was well worn already. We always had secondhand clothes, probably from Eunice's own daughters as she never threw anything away. Sarah's was green and Charlotte's blue.

One night, fairly soon after I'd moved in, Eunice came up to my bedroom and stood in the doorway watching me. I was probably prancing around the room in my pink nightie.

'Right. You're obviously not tired. I'll make you tired,' she said, and yanked me roughly out of the room. I was utterly shocked. Where was I going? Without speaking, Eunice pulled me to the top of the stairs. Was she going to push me down?

'You're to walk up and down these stairs all night. I mean all night. Right the way through.'

I looked up at her mean, hard face. She had to be joking. It was dark and cold, I had bare feet and no dressing gown. Charlotte was in bed, as were Robert, Thomas and Sarah. But now I came to think of it, I'd seen Sarah walking up and down the stairs one night just after I moved in and had wondered then what on earth was going on. I hadn't asked her as I was too scared, and she would have been too scared to answer me, anyway.

'Go on, what are you waiting for?'

I started walking down the stairs to the bottom, Eunice watching my every step. At the bottom I turned, I suppose half hoping she'd relent. I looked up at her, pleadingly.

'Come back up, this instant.'

I went back up the stairs, my little legs already aching. At the top Eunice simply gestured silently for me to go back down again. I couldn't believe this was happening to me. I carried on walking up and down, up and down, up and down until Eunice eventually went to bed and the house fell silent.

As I walked up and down like a tiny robot in the dark, I could hear the house noises. I cried pretty much most of the night. What would my mum and dad say if they knew? What would my teachers say? It seemed so utterly unjust. My legs felt leaden and my feet and ankles ached. My eyes grew heavy and I just wanted to lie down. I was cold, shivery and thirsty and I desperately needed to sleep.

As the night wore on I started to trip up because I'd lose concentration, even consciousness, from time to time. I started to hallucinate with tiredness. I'd suddenly see an image of Eunice in my face snapping 'Go to bed' at me. Then I'd come to, having fallen momentarily asleep, and find myself standing up in the hall, wondering what on earth I was doing there in my nightie in the dead of night? Then, with a jolt, I'd remember my instructions and start heaving my little legs up and down the stairs again, over and over, getting more and more exhausted, more and more confused, and feeling desolate inside.

This happened on many occasions. One time I found myself back in bed – I must have climbed back in automatically in the middle of walking up and down stairs all night. Suddenly, I was wide awake and aware of Eunice's huge face, inches from mine. She grabbed my arm, pulled me up by the hair and put me back at the top of the stairs, telling me to start walking. Confused and half asleep, I nearly fell down the whole flight.

Eunice's other night-time treat was to make me stand up all night. And I mean stand up. All night. Without moving. This was worse than going up and down stairs. Eunice would sometimes stand me in the hall, next to a weird heater system that blew out hot air when it was turned on. At night it was turned off, but it would still make strange and creepy clicking and whirring noises. I'd get very dizzy and disorientated standing up all night and would begin to hallucinate, imagining things, seeing weird images. Sometimes I'd think someone was there, then I'd blink, and they weren't.

Eunice would go off to bed and leave me there, shivering in the dark, all alone. But every so often she'd appear, checking that I was still standing there. Sometimes I would have curled up on a pile of washing in a laundry basket and she'd pull me roughly awake and onto my feet again and snap that I had to wake up and stand there to get back into her Good Books. So I'd go back to standing in the hall, listening to the clicking and whirring noises of the heater – I suppose it was something of interest – desperately trying not to fall asleep. After I'd fallen asleep a couple of times on the job, Eunice upped the stakes and made me stand at the top of the stairs, rather than at the bottom. That was terrifying because if I fell asleep I would obviously fall downstairs. Sometimes I just wanted to let go and fall because at least then I'd probably be knocked out and I'd have a legitimate reason to be asleep. But I would have to strain to keep awake, swaying at the top of the stairs, fearing what would happen if I fell down or moved.

One time during the first eighteen months, Eunice took us away for a short camping break to a folk festival at a place called Towersey. Even though it was a kind of a holiday, her punitive regime continued and we still had to strive to be in her Good Books.

We were staying in a big blue tent with two rooms in it – one room for Eunice, one room for all of us children – so there were obviously no stairs available for walking up and down. Instead, she made me run round the field three times in the pitch dark in my nightie. She was always very creative when it came to finding an alternative or extension to one of her barmy punishments.

We didn't have lilos to sleep on or anything like that – they were too expensive (and we weren't worth the expense, obviously). So we lay on roll-out bed mats, which were a bit hard and cold to sleep on. Anyway, it didn't really matter, as I was a very heavy sleeper and once I actually got to sleep, it was very difficult indeed to bring me back. I wonder now if sleep was a kind of escape from the ghastliness of being awake. I was told by the others that I would talk in my sleep, so even then, I must have been quite disturbed.

Anyway, during this stay there was a very heavy storm one night. The tent leaked and soaked my bed. When I woke up, I was wet through. I was now in her Bad Books as a consequence. Eunice said I was a stupid idiot for not waking up when the rain came in so my punishment was to stand up all night, every night in the tent for the rest of the holiday. But this happened to all of us on that trip, in turn, so each of us would have to stand up all night at some time. While I was standing up in our tent in the dark, trying to make the hours pass quicker, I would notice when Eunice had gone to sleep herself. Sometimes I would sneak back into bed, curl up and doze, but the minute I heard any movement I would spring to my feet and pretend I'd been standing there all the time. I had to be vigilant even through a dark night in a tent on a so-called holiday.

Back at George Dowty Drive another incident 'taught me a lesson' for being such a heavy sleeper. One night I fell out of bed and landed on top of a plastic toy garage. I liked playing with cars and the garage was a special thing to me. Being fast asleep, I must have hit the garage with my full, dead weight and I chipped off the plastic, which snapped, and a big chunk of it ended up embedded in my bottom. However, I must have climbed back into bed without really surfacing. In the morning I awoke, feeling very achy, and was amazed to find myself in a bed soaked with blood. The sheets were crimson and I was completely terrified. It was as if I'd been stabbed in the night.

I went to find Eunice and I said I'd cut myself, expecting her to know what to do. She looked at me with barely suppressed irritation and lifted up the back of my nightie, which was soaked through with blood. 'Oh, you fell out of bed,' was all she said. I automatically said 'No' because I was used to denying things I was accused of, just in case I got immediate, senseless punishment. It was always best to deny anything and hope for the best. However, we went back to the bedroom and Eunice pointed to my now damaged garage. She said I was stupid for not feeling anything, as if it was all my fault. Falling out of bed and cutting myself like that wasn't normal, she said coldly, while pulling off my blood-soaked sheets to change them. I was decidedly in her Bad Books and she did not tend my wound, which hurt like hell.

By then I should have known better than to expect any sympathy from Eunice when I was hurt. I was so used to being hurt by her that when I hurt myself it was just another example, in her eyes, of how inherently stupid and bad I really was. She never missed an opportunity to repeat her mantra of how evil, naughty or stupid I was, so no matter how hard I tried to be in her Good Books, I inevitably ended up in her Bad Books, which, for many years to come, meant violent punishment.

CHAPTER 9: *Beaten*

That harsh tap on the lip, when I was shooting my mouth off about seeing Charlotte's brothers and sisters at the swimming pool turned out to be the first of many. But soon these escalated into clouts, then regular beatings.

What was Eunice's aim? To shut us up? To create total, instant obedience? I think it was to break our spirits, to tame us, as a ringmaster does with wild animals. Or maybe it was to stop us thinking at all. To prevent us from being individuals or from having any personal power.

One of Eunice's favourite things to do to all the 'Bad' children (Sarah, Thomas and I) was to press her heavy, adult hand on our lips so that our teeth cut our mouths on the inside. My lips would bleed and swell up, but it was a fairly effective way of shutting me up. She would also throw things at our faces – aiming particularly for our mouths – like cans of food, books or anything that came to hand. Eunice actually knocked out Sarah's front teeth with a tin of baked beans, and then lied to the dentist, saying Sarah had fallen over.

But more commonly she would just lash out, quickly and effectively, with a smack across the mouth, splitting the skin. I have many little scars around the mouth from these everyday, common assaults and one particularly visible one from having a full tin of baked beans thrown at my face. I also have a kink in my nose (which looks as if it was probably broken at some point) sustained in one of Eunice's heavy-handed clouts around the head. The first time this happened it hurt a lot and I obviously cried and protested. But I learned very quickly that the more I protested, the worse things got. She would double her efforts and hit you even harder to shut you up.

Eunice spent years perfecting her means of shutting children up and trying to squeeze absolute obedience, literally, out of them, making them suffer in silence as much as she could. Even Judith was clearly cowed by Eunice, although she was a tall, grown woman. She once told me we had it easy as she'd been horsewhipped regularly when they had had ponies when she was little. This only goes to show how psychologically scarred and beaten Judith was. Yet she was no slouch either when it came to meting out corporal punishment. She made us drink washing-up liquid and clouted us just like her mother. Eunice often made Judith hold us when she beat us, too.

Eunice would try to strangle me and the other Bad children. She would stride swiftly towards me, pinning me down with her beady grey eyes, then suddenly her large hand would be wrapped around my throat. She'd hold me tight by the neck and squeeze very hard, but not enough to stop me breathing entirely. She was clever and usually knew when to stop. I could still breathe, just, but only very raspingly.

My first reaction would be to try to fight her off. It's natural – when someone is trying to stop you breathing, you struggle, you fight for air. But Eunice would rise to the challenge and scream at me, inches from my face, 'Relax, relax, you can breathe.' Relax! Was she joking? How can you relax when someone is trying to squeeze the life out of you? So, I would freak out, pushing against her, thrashing around while she held onto my throat, that hard, concentrated gleam in her eye. I'd think, *She's going to kill me* or *I'm dying.* But the more I struggled the harder she squeezed. So, eventually, I learned to quieten down, hold still and accept what she was doing, allowing her to terrify me into compliance.

The strangling was something she kept up her sleeve for when she really wanted to get my attention for something I'd obviously done wrong according to her Big Book of Misdemeanours. As with all her punishments, her objective was to break my spirit; once this was achieved she simply lost interest and stalked off, job done.

Although the food at Eunice's house had been seemingly plentiful at first, it became increasingly meagre once I lived there full-time. For instance, Eunice would allow us only four slices of processed bread a day. Flimsy white sliced bread. Four slices, no more, no less. It was yet another one of her arbitrary yet rigid rules. But children get hungry and their appetites vary from day to day depending on whether they are growing or sick, whether it's hot or cold weather, if they've been physically active or any number of other factors. They might want one slice of bread when they're not particularly hungry or maybe six, even eight if they're ravenous. It's just common sense.

However, if we were found to have helped ourselves to any food that was not allocated to us we would get beaten. And not just a tap or a slap, but what I called a 'proper beaten-style' beating.

Although I got away from Eunice when I went to school, I carried her rules in my head wherever I went and I would be fraught with fear about getting them wrong or doing something that she would not approve of, or worse, violently punish me for.

When Eunice doled out here punishments it was never in temper. It was always done in a cold, hard, calculating and clinical way. It was sadistic. She would say, 'I'm going to punish you now,' then there would be a wait. It might be ten minutes or it might be an hour, or when we got somewhere else, like home, if I'd been at school. It could even be ten hours later, the next day or the next week, way after the so-called misdemeanour was past. But it was noted, and the punishment would always come. This meant I'd be on edge, my stomach churning as I waited. It was never just over with quickly, but hung over me like a huge, dark cloud until she was ready to let rip.

Then she would grab me by the arm, drag me into the living room and close the door. While I stood trembling in the middle of the room, she would go and get a piece of wood that she kept under the stairs with her Jehovah's Witness books. It was about two feet long – I think it was the handle off an old copper saucepan or something.

'Take your shoes and socks off,' she would command.

If I hesitated for a second, I knew she'd get even angrier, so I'd crouch down or bend over and take them off. If I had tights on, they would have to come off, or if I had trousers on, I'd roll the legs up.

Eunice would stand beside me, patiently, while I did this. She would be holding the wooden stick in her right hand and tapping it on her left palm, as if testing its weight.

Then we would stand there, side by side in the dingy living room. She would wait to see if I cried or trembled and I would try my utmost to shut down and not show her anything.

I remember the first time it happened. I had no idea exactly what she was going to do and just stood there trembling. Suddenly, Eunice bent over, as if she was going to plant something, and I felt an enormous 'clunk' across the toes of my right foot. The pain seared through my bare feet and it felt like someone had chopped them with an axe. It was agony. I couldn't help screaming.

'Be quiet. Don't fuss. You'll make it worse for yourself.'

How could it be worse? I was shaking and crying with pain, but Eunice was bent double again, raising the stick and now she was going at my toes with great, unrelenting clunks. Clunk, clunk, clunk . . . on and on, five, ten, fifteen times. Then she changed foot.

'Stand still, you'll make it worse,' she said again.

By now I was beside myself, yelping and screaming. But there was no let-up until, finally, the punishment was done and I was left shocked and crying. A few times after being punished like this I'd ask Eunice for a hug and she would briefly put her arms round me. For a moment I would feel comforted. I had been punished and now my 'mummy' was showing that although I'd been bad, she did still love me. It was twisted and makes me feel sick now but children need affection so much they will ask for it even from their abuser.

Once, when time was short, she whacked me with the wood over my shoes; when I tried to get my shoes and socks off later that day they were glued to my feet with congealed blood. My feet were a terrible mess. Of course, I never received any treatment at the time and, to be honest, I probably said nothing about it as I knew there would be no sympathy and certainly no visit to a doctor or hospital.

A toe beating could be prompted by something trivial like

lying or something more serious, like stealing. Or it could be something imagined – something Eunice was convinced I'd done, whether or not I had. Oddly, in the early days at school I did go through a phase of hoarding all the school scissors, board rubbers and other things that I could find and putting them in my school bag. I've got no idea why I did it, but the teacher found out, and I was told off. I got a thorough beating across the toes for it when I got home. Another punishable offence was when I actually forged Eunice's signature in my little blue school text book. I had to do spelling and tables tests at school and I was scared I wouldn't be able to do it. Eunice had to sign my homework book to prove I'd been practising and I was too scared to ask her for it, because she'd test me and I was terrified of her. I had to read out the answers while I wrote them down in front of her and I didn't want to experience the consequences if I got anything wrong. So I forged her signature and she found out because the teacher could tell it was an obvious forgery. I got a nasty toe beating for that.

After these beatings my toes would be black and blue all over. I remember once at the swimming baths – before Eunice had put an end to those outings – one of the dads noticed my bruised toes and asked, 'How did you do that, then?' I just said, 'Something fell on my feet,' of course. Even in those early days I knew somehow that I was not supposed to tell the truth about Eunice's behaviour. Yet, that was so ironic given that the beatings were so often because I was accused of not having told her the truth. This meant that I had to double-think everything all of the time, presenting one story to Eunice for her satisfaction and another to the 'world' in my life outside.

Another thing at this time is that Eunice stopped me having school dinners which I liked – probably because of the cost – and began to give me a packed lunch that consisted of a bit of iceberg lettuce, a slice of cucumber and a bit of tomato. There was no bread, so there was nothing filling in my lunch. I hated salad, like most kids, so being bored with having it every day, come rain or shine, I put it in the bin quite regularly. However, one of the children who was watching me from the house – probably Charlotte – saw me do it, and reported back to Eunice. So I had another beating for being ungrateful and wasteful.

We children were not set up to be a happy household, to support and trust each other or to comfort one another when things got tough. No, we were set up as enemies from the start. We were to watch and monitor, then dob each other in to save our own skins. It made us almost feral, forcing us to fight our own corners, putting ourselves and our own survival first.

In the hierarchy Charlotte and Robert came first, and the rest of us were to serve them. One day there were six pieces of bread on the table at tea time, and only five of us there. Thomas, being a boy, was always hungry and was eyeing up the extra slice. Charlotte, however, who always had a big appetite, also had her eye on the bread. Thomas made a move to pick up the slice

'Mummy, Thomas is taking my bread,' whined Charlotte.

Thomas had hardly touched it, but Eunice, infuriated, picked up a nearby can and threw it at Thomas's head. It hit him near the eyebrow and blood started trickling down his cheek.

Not missing a beat, Charlotte picked up the slice of bread and started munching.

'That'll teach you to be greedy,' said Eunice, not offering any help. I tried to give him a tissue for the blood, but Eunice snarled at me, 'And you'll do as you're told. Sit down until I tell you to move.'

Cowed, I didn't move, but inside I was seething, not only at Charlotte's provocative behaviour, but also because Thomas was hurt and I could do nothing to help him. Sarah just sat with her head down, trying to be 'good', while Robert was largely oblivious to what was going on. He was only a toddler and was off in his own little world.

At first the beatings and other vile punishments really hurt. My eyes would fill with tears and I'd feel overwhelmed by pain and indignation. My face would flush with anger and humiliation and I would try to escape her iron grasp. But Eunice was determined to beat me – all of us – into submission so I had to pretend to give in to make her satisfied. I'd be counting the cracks in the wall and thinking, *It'll be over in a minute, if you just hold still.* In the end I Iearned to blank out, to numb my feelings, to detach from my body, to go somewhere else within myself until the punishment was done. I learned to simply switch off and endure.

That was the only way to survive. Or so I thought.

CHAPTER 10: *The Farm*

Eunice had a grand plan. I truly believe that she cleverly, calculatedly and coldly devised her plan – actually a scam – and then enacted it, methodically, over a period of time, taking us children with her as her unwilling entourage.

Eunice had seen an opportunity to acquire some more property for herself – a second home in the country – without having to buy it. There is absolutely no doubt in my mind about this. Although she was quick to denounce me, Thomas and Sarah as evil, she was more devious than any of us. She accused us of what was actually true of herself. She was up to no good, but she covered it up and hoped, as always, to pull the wool not only over our eyes, but over our entire heads, too.

Unbeknown to us, Eunice had begun to befriend an elderly man called John Drake who owned a farm near an affluent, pretty market town called Pershore, north of Tewkesbury. I think she met him after fruit picking on his farm some time before we knew her and had somehow kept in touch. She must have made a mental note to go back and groom him in the same way as she had my parents: she could see a niche and would fill it when there was something in it for her. John had never married and he didn't have any children and was now living alone.

The first time we met John was on a May bank holiday in 1994. Eunice packed us up in her Volvo Estate and we drove off into the country for about half an hour until we reached a bend in a leafy road. We all piled out and went through a big crossbar gate, past a large, rambling red-bricked Victorian farmhouse with neatly trimmed lawns and huge trees. A selection of vehicles was parked around the various outhouses.

A man in a flat cap welcomed us. He had yellowish, salt-and-pepper hair, wore those typical baggy tweed trousers with braces and smelled of sweat. John Drake was not a healthy man. He was a heavy smoker with a hacking cough who breathed heavily and wheezed noticeably all the time. He was very small, with a red face, and looked ancient to me.

That sunny spring day he gave us all little cardboard punnets and we ran off down the field. John Drake grew raspberries, gooseberries, blackcurrants, redcurrants, broad beans, corn and he had an orchard loaded with apples in the autumn. That first day we picked raspberries, which was a real treat, especially because when we picked the fruit, we could eat it. It felt like the most fantastic freedom in our heavily constrained lives. I'd never seen fruit growing before and it was wonderful to pluck the red berries from the bush and cram the sweet, juicy fruit into my mouth. We had more fun than I could remember, and even Charlotte seemed nice that sunny afternoon. We even laughed and skipped around, just like ordinary kids would do.

After that we went on several more trips to the farm and we got to know John, as Eunice began to familiarize him with us all. I remember we had dinner there a few times, cooked entirely by John (which made a change from Eunice's cooking). He made delicious food like roast lamb with all the trimmings and although he was a fairly grumpy individual, I felt he was being generous towards us. Especially when he made us kids a blancmange or jelly and ice cream served up with some of his home-grown fruit.

Soon we were swinging back and forth regularly between George Dowty and the farm, sometimes staying overnight, just sleeping on cushions pulled off the sofa onto the floor in the living room. Eunice told us firmly to be very quiet. Again, another place where we couldn't make any noise.

John Drake was a typical, hard-working bachelor farmer, who had lived with his mother on the family farm until she'd died a few years earlier. He kept a shrine to her, so I guess they were very close and he'd nursed her when she was sick until her death. Eckington Bank Farm had been John's life's work and had probably been in his family for at least two generations. I got the feeling that he had worked from dawn till dusk, constantly outside in all weathers, but that now his mother was gone, he was leading a fairly lonely existence. That was, until Eunice came along, with her gaggle of assorted waifs and strays in tow.

The massive house, with all its rambling rooms, had an old man's smell. It wasn't heated, but had a big, black Raeburn in the kitchen, used for the hot water as well as the cooking.

We usually entered the house through the back door, into a washroom. From there you could go into a large, chilly sun lounge to the left or the huge kitchen to the right. I noticed John only had a tiny fridge, and there wasn't a freezer. Instead, there was an old-fashioned larder off the kitchen, which he used to store cans of baked beans and stewing steak, instant coffee, hot chocolate and tins of biscuits.

The house was very rundown with a generally threadbare look about it. Overall, it was pretty dirty and John didn't do much to clean it up. There was a long strip of tatty greenish carpet running through the hall, which was huge. The living room, off the hall, had a dingy old, leafy green fitted carpet in it and a Welsh dresser. Another reception room, which he used as a lounge, had a wooden floor and a dusty old scatter rug.

In contrast with the inside of the house, the outside was John's pride and joy. Outside the back door there was an old table with a Formica covering, a grubby chequered white and blue tablecloth, and a big old-fashioned set of scales where he used to weigh the fruit. Beyond the table was a big, flat acre of green lawn, a pond in a corner with ducks and geese swimming about and, beyond that, an enormous corrugated iron barn which had a strange, old-fashioned potato-sorting machine in it. There were brick and wooden outhouses to the left, including a black chicken shed and old cars in the grounds to the left of the main lawn: John's was an old yellow Ford Escort with two doors. Beyond the big barn with the potato sorter were fields stretching way into the distance. To the right of the farm was another huge, well-kept lawn, hidden behind trees and hedges and the local churchyard beyond, full of gravestones.

One bizarre aspect of Eunice's 'friendship' with John Drake was that he hated Jehovah's Witnesses. He utterly despised them. Eunice would exhort us not to mention them – on pain of punishment of course – which seemed weird to me. If she was such a strong believer, why would she be such good friends with a man who hated Jehovah's Witnesses? The answer was pretty clear. Eunice had attached herself to a man who was lonely and, as we soon found out, terminally sick. It turned out he had lung cancer and needed a major operation. Eunice must have found this out pretty quickly and offered, selfless angel of mercy that she was, to help him out. I can imagine her wooing him: 'It's all right, John. I'll come over and look after you. The kids will love helping out on the farm.' Indeed, not only would we help, but soon we'd be doing every aspect of hard labour possible, as part of Eunice's grand scheme to inherit the farm from poor, unsuspecting John Drake.

There was a transitional period of several months during which we were living between George Dowty Drive – which Eunice still owned and never sold – and Eckington Bank. I think it was early autumn when, without explaining anything to us, Eunice took us to the farm to stay full-time. Just like that. Judith was left at George Dowty a lot of the time, along with the baby, and there was still a lot of swinging back and forth between the two houses, which were only about a half an hour or forty minutes' drive apart, depending on the traffic. But Charlotte, Sarah, Thomas and I were deposited on the farm and a new life began.

When we first went over to live at the farm John Drake had just come out of hospital, following major surgery for his lung cancer. Eunice was there, I suppose, to look after him. She'd probably persuaded him she was a nurse – of sorts – and she even slept in his room with him. I don't think there was any hanky panky going on; I think she was simply trying to woo him, to make him feel cared for, and then, obviously, indebted. She had her eye set on the ultimate prize: ownership of the farm.

In the daytime, John would sit in the lounge in an electric chair that tipped backwards at the press of a button, so he could rest. Eunice told us to be quiet as church mice, as he was sick and recovering, so we would go outside and wander about.

At first it seemed the move might even improve things for us. We had a slight whiff of freedom, being allowed to explore the fields, the trees and the woods beyond. I liked looking at the little graveyard over the low drystone wall, peering at the inscriptions on all the wonky headstones. There were mini-tractors, as I called them (they were really lawnmowers), which we had fun playing on. I would spend hours on them, pretending I was riding a beautiful pony or dreaming about going on a sunny holiday. I was always fantasizing. John was nice enough to let us play on them and although he was grumpy, he never harmed us – unlike our so-called foster mother.

At the bottom of the field there were a couple of small black sheds in which, we were told, a hermit had lived at one time. That seemed quite magical and although they were out of bounds, I would imagine who had lived there and what magical powers he might have had.

The other good thing about the farm, for me, was the animals. There were ducks, geese, chickens, cats and later black pigs and a dog, which would become my friends, in time. I was very happy having animals to talk to, especially when things got tough.

The pecking order among us children remained the same

as it had been at George Dowty. Charlotte, who was always Eunice's favourite, was given a bed upstairs, in a room of her own. She was treated like a little princess and although she did endure some of the same punishments as us, they were not as severe. I remember Eunice slapping her leg or taking away her pocket money (the rest of us didn't have any to start with), but she always had some privileges, too, like her own bed or toys, which made me dislike her a lot. We three – Sarah, Thomas and I – were the 'Baddies' and had to sleep on the draughty wooden floor, on smelly old cushions pulled off the sofa, in the living room. We didn't have bedding but would grab an old blanket or eiderdown and wrap it around ourselves. I thought this was temporary, at first, but it became a way of life for a very long time.

Although many things were now different, the bizarre regime of daily rituals and punishments established at George Dowty went on as usual. The compulsory breakfast of All-Bran and linseeds followed by toilet inspections (now in an outhouse, away from John Drake's view) and enemas if we didn't perform adequately were still enforced. Washing-up liquid down the throat for lying or backchatting, strangleholds to teach us a lesson and daily clouts around the head, slaps on the mouth and punches for any minor misdemeanour continued as before. There were still Good Books and Bad Books, depending on which way the wind was blowing, and the prospect of a 'proper beaten-style' beating if we were in Eunice's Bad Books. Plus, we were still made to stand up all night if we didn't go to sleep on time. However, Eunice did stop us walking up and down stairs at this time, for a while at least, as the stairs creaked and I don't think she wanted to alert John to her bizarre and cruel treatment. It was certainly not a case of her softening towards us; quite the opposite.

At first, Eunice had to be fairly quiet and our punishments were meted out once John was fast asleep in the lounge. He was on medication, I guess morphine for pain, so Eunice knew full well when to exact her punishments out of earshot. Also, with plenty of outhouses, Eunice had other places she could take us to, where, if we made a noise, we were too far away for John, or anyone else for that matter, to hear.

As for school, it soon became clear that my school back in Tewkesbury was too far away for us to commute daily. I was doing well at school and really loved it. I remember saying to my friends and teacher just before half term, 'See you next week, after the break', as I was always keen to return. I thought I'd be back like everyone else. Instead I was taken out of school abruptly. Although I could have transferred to another school near by, Eunice could not be bothered with any of that. It didn't suit her plan at all. Instead Eunice applied to be the home tutor for Thomas and me (and later Robert), which, I eventually discovered, involved nothing more than her writing a letter to the local education authority.

As she was already home tutoring Charlotte and Sarah, it was probably easy for her to argue that she could run a little home school for all the children in her care.

Now we were living in Pershore we came under Worcestershire County Council and whenever an inspector visited, Eunice was able to put on a show worthy of Mary Poppins. She'd always receive warning that he was coming and would get us all cleaning. For once she'd be tidy and things would shine. She'd buy us new books and we'd be sitting at the table, writing, with clean hair and scrubbed faces, when the inspector called. Once they were gone, things returned to normal, of course.

By tutoring us at home she succeeded in removing me from any sort of normal life and contact with the outside world. We slowly but surely became trapped on the farm, our only outings being to Jehovah's Witness meetings to which Eunice still dragged us regularly (if not quite as often as at George Dowty), usually under cover of darkness and without John knowing. Again we were sworn to silence, on pain of something horrible happening to us.

We were isolated and shut off and although, at first, it seemed to some extent that living on the farm would be a little like going on holiday, we hadn't banked on how having total control over us would gradually intensify Eunice's warped behaviour. Having effectively cut me off from the outside world it would no longer matter so much where my bruises or cuts were, how shabbily I would be dressed or whether I got enough to eat.

About this time Eunice decided to get a dog. He was a lovely, black Labrador puppy called Jet and, of course, it fell to me to train him. I like animals, but I didn't really know much about dogs, and I'd certainly never trained one, so it was yet another duty I had to do on top of everything else. However, I was happy to give it a go, as a dog was a companion of sorts. He was also to be some kind of guard-dog, as the farm was pretty exposed, being by the side of the road on the outskirts of the village, and people knew John Drake was very poorly by then and couldn't protect the farm like he used to.

The puppy would sleep in a basket under the kitchen table and Eunice would often tell me to sleep with him. I would curl up on the floor, under the table, on a cushion, with a blanket over me – just like a dog, too. I'm sure she wanted me to sleep with him to stop him crying as puppies always whine when they're left alone at night. Again, it was all about Eunice and her comfort, as she hated to be disturbed and disliked noise. It was draughty and uncomfortable on the cold red and white quarry tiles of the kitchen floor, but in a way it was quite nice to sleep with the dog. I guess I felt I could relate to him.

I knew nothing about housetraining a puppy and, of course, at first he would wee and poo all over the place. One morning Eunice came into the kitchen and found that Jet had done his business in the night by the back door while I was asleep. Eunice was furious.

'Get up,' she snapped. I crawled out from under the table, tired and dishevelled. Eunice's jaw was set, which meant trouble.

'What's this?'

Eunice pointed to a little puddle by the back door with a small brown sausage of dog poo beside it. She marched over and stared down at it accusingly. Jet sat, wagging his tail, tongue out, panting, oblivious, looking pleased with himself. I tried to disappear into the shadows of the kitchen, not knowing what Eunice might do next.

'Come here!'

It was me, not the dog, she was commanding. Eunice was glaring at me with her dead, grey eyes, her thin mouth clamped in a mask of disapproval. I crept over to stand next to her, head down, my legs feeling weak. *What was she going to do now?* Suddenly she grabbed me by the back of my hair and forced me to my knees, which hurt as they hit the unforgiving tiled floor. Inches from my face were the pile of dog poo and the pool of wee, glistening in the morning light. Slowly, Eunice pushed my head further down. The stench of the poo entered my nostrils, turning my stomach and then, with a sudden further push, my face was in it. The wet, stinky mass was squishing up my nostrils, over my cheeks and eyelids and I had to fight it from going into the corners of my mouth. Eunice pushed my face into the mess and rubbed it back and forth, round and round. I desperately squeezed my eyes and mouth shut, although I could feel the poo oozing up my nostrils. I couldn't breathe as I couldn't open my mouth and my nose was full of lumpy globs of dog mess. Finally, after a good minute, she stopped and I was released. I stood up, spluttering, my face covered with poo. I automatically put my hands up to wipe my mouth and nose but Eunice swatted my hand away.

'Don't wipe it off.'

I opened my mouth to breathe, but could now taste the poo on my tongue and lips. I wanted to be sick, but I wouldn't let myself. Not in front of *her*. I started shaking involuntarily.

'That's how you teach dogs not to poo. You rub their faces in it. Got it?'

I said nothing, still struggling not to vomit as the revolting stench of dog poo filled my every pore.

'Don't take it off until I say.'

With that Eunice marched out of the kitchen, leaving me standing there and Jet staring up at me, head on one side, totally bemused.

Over the next months, this 'dog training' happened a few times more, when Jet had an 'accident', although I always tried desperately hard to get him out the back door in time. It wasn't easy to get him to stop pooing round the house, as he was only a baby, plus I wasn't always with him because I also had Robert to look after, too. However, after a while, if I was asleep with Jet under the table, I'd automatically wake up so I could pop him out in the middle of the night to wee. Luckily, by the time he was a year old he was finally trained and my own 'dog training' also stopped. I'd certainly learned another painful lesson at Eunice's hands.

CHAPTER 11: *Imprisoned*

Because Charlotte was Eunice's favourite I was given all sorts of household chores to do instead of her as if I, and not she, was the eldest child. One of my responsibilities was making sure that Eunice had a list of what food and general supplies we needed, well in advance of things running out. It was hard for me, at nine, to work out what weekly provisions were needed for two adults and five kids, let alone the animals. With something like chicken feed, for instance, Eunice told me I had to give her a three-day warning before it ran out. I had to check the cupboards, the larder and the fridge, plus all the animal feed, and make sure she knew if things were running low. Eunice said she was too busy herself as she was looking after John, who was in terminal decline by then.

One day I forgot to tell her about the chicken feed, but I was so terrified I didn't dare say anything. I counted down each day – three, two, one – until it was too late.

Eunice came into the kitchen and looked around with a grim expression. I knew that look and I tried to sneak past her, out of the door. She grabbed me by the hair and pulled me back.

'Oh, no you don't.' She turned me round to face her, digging her scrawny fingers into my shoulders. 'Where is it?'

I feigned innocence and just looked ahead of me, stony-faced. It was all I could think to do, but my heart was racing under my pink and white spotted T-shirt. By now, Charlotte and Sarah had crept to the kitchen door and were watching.

Eunice did not like being ignored. She bent forwards and said menacingly, 'Where's the chicken feed?'

'I . . . er . . .'

I tried to speak, but my voice trailed off. I could smell the terrible odour of her armpits as it wafted up to me; being close to her was always revolting. Her eyes were boring into me and I had no idea what she'd do next.

'Right, that's it.' Eunice yanked me by the arm out of the kitchen and into the living room. In front of the grate there was a crowbar on the slate; she bent over and picked it up. Until now she'd hit my feet with a variety of sticks – old table legs, ends of copper bed pans, bits of beading, indeed, whatever came to hand. I knew that my tiny feet would not hold up against a crowbar.

I stood shivering in the middle of the room, anticipating the pain.

'How many times have I told you to let me know three days in advance? I can't just drop everything and go running out to the shops for chicken feed willy nilly. It's your responsibility.'

Eunice stood in front of me, but I tried to avoid her eyes. I focused on a large crack in the wall that went from the side of the fireplace up to the ceiling. I had flimsy shoes on and I kicked them off.

Eunice savoured the moment, holding the heavy crowbar in her right hand. Suddenly she bent over and I gritted my teeth and focused as hard as I could on the crack in the wall.

Clunk. Clunk.

Oh God, the pain was violent and immediate. I bit my lip, trembling uncontrollably; tears ran down my cheeks.

Clunk. Clunk.

The other foot was hit and the pain enveloped me instantly. It was so bad I felt sick instantly and wanted to fall over and scream, but I suppressed as much as I could, biting deeper into my lower lip. I stared maniacally at the crack in the wall, following its feathery tracks upwards and sideways towards the dingy ceiling. I was really shaking now as the shock took over.

'I don't think you'll be forgetting again, you little scum.'

With that, Eunice strode out of the room and I collapsed on the floor, crying uncontrollably at last. My feet felt like they'd been mashed to pieces in a farm machine and I couldn't stand up. They were swollen and already bruising (I think it was possible that my toe was broken, although I can't be sure) and for several days afterwards I could only hobble around.

Another onerous job I had was to look after Robert. He was now a toddler, although he was still in nappies. He was becoming quite hyperactive and was very tricky to manage. I was given the primary responsibility of caring for him, day and night. I had to tend to him, change his nappy, feed, wash and clothe him and – once Jet was trained – sleep with him. I had to keep him amused and out of trouble all day, so I often ended up walking him round and round the fields just to wear him out, which was exhausting. He slept in a cot in the living room with me, Sarah and Thomas.

Eunice would give Robert bottles of 7UP to drink, even at night. Not water or milk, but loads of fizzy, sweetened pop. My job was to give him three seven-ounce bottles of 7UP overnight. No wonder he was hyperactive with all those E-numbers, additives and sugar sloshing around in him. I trying to change his nappy one night when he was so hyped up he was bucking around and poo went everywhere. I got a clout around the head for that, then had my face pushed into his nappy, just like with Jet's 'potty training'. It was disgusting and it was entirely my fault, of course.

John Drake was now very poorly and Eunice was hot on her campaign to have the farm signed over to her. She was quite brazen about it at times, which surprised me, saying things like, 'If you're too noisy we'll never get him to give us the farm'.

To please John (and, of course, to ensure her inheritance was safe) we had to be quiet, day and night. This was one of the reasons we weren't allowed upstairs (except for Charlotte, her 'princess'). We all had to tiptoe around, which was doubly difficult with Robert being so hyperactive. It was a real strain to keep him calm and I was only a child myself, so I had no real authority.

As I mentioned earlier, I was a heavy sleeper and it was difficult to wake me once I was asleep. One night Robert started crying, calling out for his 'mummy' (meaning Eunice, of course); he must have been wailing good and proper but I didn't hear a thing even though he was in the same room as me. I was curled up on a sofa cushion, an old smelly duvet wrapped under and over me, dead to the world. Suddenly, I was being pulled up onto my feet and out of bed. Eunice was in an ice-cold rage and was spitting fury at me. It was blatantly obvious what she was angry about, and it certainly wasn't the baby's welfare.

'You've really upset John Drake now – we won't get the house and it'll be your fault.'

I said nothing, as I was confused and terrified by being woken up in this way. Robert continued screaming as well, so there was chaos. Eunice dragged Sarah to her feet too and barked at her to comfort the baby. I thought that might be it, but Eunice had other plans for me that night. She pulled me out of the back door by my hair, barefoot and still in my nightie, then frog-marched me to the big barn across the lawn. *I'm really in for it now*, I thought. I suppose I expected a toe beating which was what I usually got when Eunice wanted to hurt me badly. But this time it seemed she had even more outrageously sadistic plans.

'Lie down,' was all she said to me.

Seeing I was not sure exactly what I should do, she indicated a spot on the floor quite near the door, next to the potato-sorting machine I'd seen the first time we looked around the barn. Although there was electricity in the barn the light was very dim and I remember looking at the four bare bulbs along the centre of the high barn ceiling. I found myself examining the wooden cogs and conveyor belts of the machine with some curiosity, while Eunice rifled in the dark corners of the barn, clearly looking for something. Then her voice broke into my night-time reverie.

'Put your leg up.'

Leg up what? For a moment I didn't know what she meant. She was standing beside me, towering over me, a stern look on her face.

'Hold your leg up. Come on,' she snapped.

I duly raised one leg in the air and it shook. I was terrified at the thought of what she might be up to now. I felt I might wee myself with fear at any moment, and knew that doing so would prompt even more punishment. I remember the floor being very hard and cold that night, as I lay there, exposed, with Eunice hovering over me, her face as black as thunder. Then suddenly, she produced a long wooden stick, which she must have found in the barn, raised it up high and brought it down hard on the bare, naked, upturned sole of my foot.

Whack.

I heard it thwack, like something was breaking. It hurt like hell and I screamed involuntarily, although I knew I was supposed to be silent. My leg moved away, also involuntarily, but she grabbed it roughly and brought it back into position, while I continued to scream and protest, trying to wriggle out from under. The sole of my foot was on fire; I couldn't believe it wasn't split open and bleeding from the pain. Meanwhile Eunice was not happy with me making a noise and she was in fierce and furious mode. She was not having any of it. She knew exactly what she wanted and how she was going to get it.

'Keep still and shut up,' she snapped. 'You'll wake John Drake.'

Then the stick came down again and I thought I'd vomit with pain.

Whack. Whack. Whack. Whack. Ten . . . twenty . . . thirty . . . forty . . .

I counted numbly as the beats rained down. I couldn't help myself and screamed again and again. But on and on and on she went.

Whack. Whack. Whack.

Tears were streaming down my face. I was sobbing helplessly, but Eunice was indifferent. She almost had a zonked-out expression, as if she was not really there, just going through the motions, like a robot. Then the other foot had to be held up – by me – and the same punishment was enacted: calmly, calculatingly, viciously. I was totally distraught. I writhed from side to side, my feet pulsating with pain, but If I tried to move away or let my leg flop, Eunice would grab my ankle roughly again and pull my leg up to a position that exposed the sole of my foot better still, so she could whack it full on with her stick.

'It'll be much worse for you if you don't stop messing around,' was all she said, in a flat, hard tone. 'I'm doing it like this so the bruises won't show.'

At one point the pain was so great that I was losing consciousness for a moment, blanking out, then coming to and staring hard at the potato-sorting machine, trying to lose myself in something. I found an odd comfort in that strange contraption. I must have realized that I had to escape in my mind to survive what was happening. I started following the lines of the conveyor belt, tracing the cogs, going round and round, endlessly, as the stick continued to come down with a sickening thud on my bare foot. Suddenly, I heard a rat behind the machine, gnawing at the wood, which freaked me out more at that moment than the fact that a fully grown woman was trying to shred the soles of my size-one feet with an implement of sheer torture.

After the beating was over, I was in pieces. I rolled over, sobbing, distraught, agonized. I could hardly breathe, I couldn't move and I wanted to die.

Eunice calmly put the stick away in a dark corner of the barn. 'Get up,' she said coldly.

Automatically, I reached my arms out towards her, wanting a hug. It was a childish gesture, made in a very desperate, primitive way, but I needed comfort – even from the woman who had just beaten me in a way I had never believed possible. Even though she had shown how much me she hated me, I still wanted her love.

But tonight, in the dank, dark barn, she ignored my outstretched arms completely. She wouldn't put her arms around me and that was that. Other times she had told me she was only punishing me 'for my own good' or to 'teach me a lesson'. This time it was different. The stakes were higher: this beating was because she wanted the farm, very badly indeed.

I lifted myself up onto my battered feet, which felt as though they'd been skinned. I found it hard to walk properly but Eunice commanded: 'Don't limp.'

Traumatized and nauseated by every tentative step, I tried to put on a brave face and hobbled as best I could out of the barn and back across the garden. Once out of her view I could limp to my heart's content, the grass cooling my mashed-up feet. I was in deep shock that night. Everything was a blur and occasional sobs surfaced as I made my way through the dark kitchen to the living room, where I had to go back to sleep on the floor. I had to remember not to make a noise, and also to resume my duties, making sure Robert didn't make a sound either. I now knew that the penalty for making so much as a whisper was more horrible than anything that had ever gone before. I don't think I'd ever felt so lonely or desolate as I did that night on the farm.

This was the new way of life now. After this first night-time trauma, we would all be forced out to the barn regularly at the slightest noise and dealt with violently (all except Charlotte and Robert, who were just slapped and clouted occasionally). Eunice kept various implements of torture in there and we children even queued up sometimes to wait for our punishment.

One thing she liked to do was to beat one of us to get at the truth – a bit like a Nazi interrogator in an old black and white film or something out of the Spanish Inquisition. She would whack one of us on the feet to see if she could make us squeal. Eunice would say things like, 'I'll beat you all until I find out who's done it,' referring to a crime like taking a slice of bread or answering back. Eunice would blame us for something as trivial as moving the chicken feed, although often one of the animals was guilty. Whatever it was, the three of us – Sarah, Thomas and I – always got the blame and the worst treatment. Sometimes I'd own up for the sake of stopping the beatings, even if it was quite obvious that none of us was guilty. Other times we'd all just stay stubbornly silent and not admit to anything. And sometimes one of us would buckle under pressure and blurt out the real culprit. However, Thomas and I would often cover for each other, and feel close, at these moments, as a consequence of Eunice's tyranny.

I remember one day I was in the garden, just playing around on the lawn, and I saw a hazelnut lying there. I picked it up, cracked it open and ate it, curious as to what it tasted like and probably a bit hungry, too. Then I carried on playing, fantasizing about goodness knows what, like I always did. When I went into the kitchen, Eunice was there, looking thunderously at me. 'What did you do?'

I had to rack my brains. What did she mean? I didn't dare say anything, but I thought hard, panicking. *What did I do? I don't know what I did. I was playing.*

'What did you do? While you were out there? I told you not to touch anything.'

What did she mean? I couldn't understand what she was getting at. Had I touched something valuable, like a farming tool? Maybe she'd got confused or something? I just didn't know. All I knew was that I'd been outside playing in the garden. I found my voice and denied any wrongdoing.

'You're a liar. I saw you.'

Her face was white with suppressed rage and I was dragged off to the barn and given the new style of beating on the soles of my feet to bash the truth out of me. She beat me for a very long time. Then, at the end of it all, she simply revealed my heinous crime in a controlled, hard voice:

'You picked up a hazelnut. I told you not to touch anything and you disobeyed me.'

Pause, while I tried to take in anything beyond the immediate agony of my pulped feet. *Oh, hell, the hazelnut.*

'You know very well that you brought it on yourself.'

I struggled to understand how this could be, as I rolled onto one side, panting with pain.

'You know I only do this because if I don't you'll die a horrible death – you know you will, if you don't become totally honest.'

Then she turned and walked out the barn, leaving me in a heap on the floor.

Another thing that happened around this time was going to hurt me for a very long time; in fact, thinking about it still upsets me today.

Eunice always cut our hair as it was obviously cheaper than taking us to a hairdresser. Plus, it meant she wouldn't have to expose us to an observant adult who might notice our cuts and bruises, especially the numerous ones on our heads and mouths.

My hair was always a bone of contention between us. I was very proud of my jet-black curly hair and liked it long. Eunice thought it was too unkempt and wild – she wanted me shorn like a sheep. She was always rough with my hair and grimaced as she brushed it – I was obviously disgusting to her. She would make me sit on an upright chair in the kitchen, with a towel around my neck, and she would roughly snip off a couple of inches of my unruly 'gypsy' hair. Of course, whenever she cut my hair, she would never consult me as to what I wanted. She would simply start hacking away, aggressively, with her sharp scissors. In fact, if I didn't keep my head in the right position, she would give me a little jab with her scissors, stabbing me in the head with the sharp points to make me sit up and pay attention. This would make me very nervous, to the point that I couldn't hold my head still. The more I tried, the more I seemed to wobble, the more she jabbed at me, which made me flinch, bringing more jabs. It was a vicious circle, literally.

One day, when I was about nine or ten, Eunice took it into her head to cut all my hair off. I didn't want her to – my hair was my identity and I loved it. It was almost as if it was the one thing that I had left which was my own. However, I knew that if she picked up on the fact that it mattered to me, she'd do it to spite me, so I tried to be as deadpan as I could.

I sat on a stool in the kitchen with Eunice standing behind me with her scissors, going snip, snip, snip. I wanted to say 'Stop' or 'Enough', but I had to sit in silence as she cut away, making my hair shorter and shorter as I helplessly watched my locks falling to the floor.

Higher and higher went her scissors, my eyes darting about to follow her fingers, and if I moved, *stab*, I'd get a steel point in the head. I could feel the tears welling up, but I bit my lip, hard. I wasn't going to show her I cared, because if I did she'd just say I was vain and cut it even shorter. This particular cut left me with about an inch of hair all over my head. I looked like a shorn and forlorn black sheep. Looking in the bathroom mirror afterwards I could see my big, hazel eyes peering out from under a curly, dark skullcap. It was all too much and I collapsed into silent tears of grief. I never would have cried about it in front of Eunice, or anyone else for that matter, as I was learning to keep my tears and misery to myself. But this felt like such a disfigurement. I had suffered and endured so much at Eunice's hands, but this was one indignity too many.

After this I would often stare at the mirror when I was alone and simply cry. But I'd never show anyone else. I didn't dare.

A few days later something snapped inside me. It was over something very trivial, but I guess it's often the small things that push us over the edge.

It was about five in the evening and I was trying to decide with Robert which video to put on the TV. We weren't allowed videos very often, but for some reason that afternoon we'd been told we could watch something. I wanted to watch

Free Willy and he wanted to watch *Budgie, The Helicopter* and, I suppose, it was one of those days when I just didn't want to give way to him, even though he was younger and favoured. Maybe I was fed up with my hair, maybe I was sick of looking after him and never having what I wanted. After all, I was only a child myself. I put on *Free Willy* first, ignoring his complaints. However, Robert continued to make a fuss and Eunice got to hear about it. She came striding in and told me I was going to be beaten for it. Later.

I knew 'later' could mean anything from half an hour to a day. The waiting and the build-up were horrible and because I knew what was coming I was totally gripped by fear. If she'd done it there and then in anger it would have been over and done with. But it was the threat, the long wait that drove me to the edge that day. I'd had enough and simply couldn't stand waiting to be hurt any more.

I remember standing in the washroom, having to take my shoes and socks off as usual and just not wanting to go through with it. It was too much to contemplate – just one beating too far. I could just about deal with Eunice's random, daily cruelty – like a clout around the head, or even a squirt of washing-up liquid in the mouth. But for some reason – maybe because I'd just watched *Free Willy*, a heart-rending film about escape and freedom – I felt I could no longer go meekly like a lamb to the slaughter.

Whatever it was, I panicked and ran out the back door of

the kitchen and down the garden. I ran and ran and ran, as fast as I could, speeding over the field, jumping over the graveyard fence to the right of the farm. I landed in brambles, got to my feet and just kept running. I ripped my T-shirt badly on the fence (that would earn yet another beating, no doubt, but I didn't care right now) and ran out across the street. I stopped and looked to the left and right. I didn't know where to go, or what to do; I just knew I had to get away.

It was midwinter, so it was pretty nippy, and I was in thin clothes and barefoot. It was early evening by then; it was dark already and I could see the lights coming on in houses around the village.

Winding country lanes surrounded the farm with houses along one side and I soon came across a cottage with a red four-by-four parked in the drive. I scrambled underneath it and just lay there on the cold cobblestones, praying and praying that nobody would come out of the cottage, and particularly that no one would get into the Jeep and start it up. I stared bleakly at the underside of the car, fascinated by all the pipes and rivets, covered by a black oily fur. I could see lights twinkling in the cottage and hear voices far off, but so far, so good.

Then I heard an engine coming. The house I was outside was only round the corner from the farm and, of course, Eunice would come looking for me, as soon as she'd discovered I'd escaped. As the car slid past the gates of the cottage, it paused briefly. I rolled sideways and peeked out and saw Eunice driving her mustard Volvo estate with Judith in the passenger seat peering out the side window towards me, flashing a torch. I held my breath and kept still, then they moved off, thankfully, without seeing me.

I rolled onto my back, uncomfortable on the hard ground. *What should I do next?* I lay for what seemed like an eternity trying to work out what to do. It was getting very dark now and the temperature was dropping, so I was really shivering. I was hungry, but I was able to suppress any pangs as I was so used to using my mind to control my body or feelings. I must have stayed under that car for about six hours or so, until I was frozen and felt sort of woozy with hunger and exhaustion.

Then suddenly, I thought of the donkeys over in the field, snug in their shed. They probably had hay and would be warm to snuggle up with. So under cover of darkness (it was now about midnight, I think), I sneaked out from my hiding place and ran down the lane and across a bridge to a little black shed behind the graveyard, where the donkeys were. It was pitch-black inside. I tiptoed in, whispering to the donkeys not to be afraid, that I wasn't going to hurt them. I was met by a warm animal smell and a waft of dung. The donkeys were in a one part of the shed but I was disappointed to see that where I had entered there wasn't any hay, only a bit of straw on a concrete floor. I was so exhausted that I simply curled up in a corner and fell into an immediate, dreamless sleep.

The next thing I knew there was a helicopter buzzing overhead. A searchlight came in through the window and I was bathed in brilliant light. I was suddenly wide awake. I heard someone's voice shouting out 'Harriet', and I thought, *How strange there's a donkey called Harriet.* I must have been delirious by then. The door was flung open and a tall policeman stood looking in at me: 'There you are, young lady. We've been looking for you everywhere. Do you know how many people are worried about you?'

Yeah, right, was all I could think. Someone threw a blanket around my shoulders and as I couldn't walk by then I was lifted up and carried out by the policeman. I was then bundled into a police car, with two Alsatians screened off in the back. The policeman told me I was suffering from hypothermia and could have died in the shed – the temperature was below zero and I had barely any clothes on. But I didn't really care; I felt so drowsy and far away.

I was surprised that the policeman drove me back to George Dowty Drive and not the farm, although I realized afterwards it was because this was where we were supposed to be living. Eunice was keeping up pretences with the police and, as usual, she was doing something on the sly. Social services had recently visited apparently and Eunice had clearly tidied the place up (it was usually a terrible tip). She'd got the police to drive me back to George Dowty Drive so her cover wasn't blown.

When we got there, Eunice was standing in the doorway waiting for me, a strange look on her face. I wondered what punishment I would get now. No doubt something doubly horrible on top of the one I'd missed to teach me another lesson.

Once the policeman had gone and the door was closed I waited for the blows, but Eunice actually made me a hot chocolate – a rare first. There were no hugs or words of comfort, but she didn't ask for an explanation, which was a relief. She just tried to guilt-trip me by saying, 'You realize you could have woken up the whole family. How do you think the baby would have felt about all this fuss?'

Eunice had left Judith at the farm with the other kids while we played 'happy families' for the sake of the police and social services. Eunice never asked me why I ran away, but the next day, as she drove me back to the farm, she said she'd let me off of the beating – *this once* – because I'd had enough punishment for that day. I didn't trust her and thought she'd beat me anyway. And I knew that even if I was let off today, there'd be another beating tomorrow, for something else. It was only a matter of time.

CHAPTER 12: *Slaves*

After being brought back to the farm, I lost all hope of escaping from Eunice. Instead of planning to run away again, I grabbed whatever moments of play, freedom or pleasure I could get. There weren't many – although Eunice did try to teach us at home, there wasn't much time for lessons as my life was mainly focused on looking after Robert, which was definitely a full-time job.

Eunice ruled all of our lives, including John Drake's, with a will of steel and it seemed that as John declined daily, Eunice's rules got harsher. For instance, she had taken to controlling the food a lot more. I'm not sure whether she was finding it expensive to run both George Dowty Drive (where Judith still lived) and the farm, with little or no financial help from John Drake, but for some reason food had begun to get very scarce. We were not allowed to help ourselves to food at all and she would dole out what she thought was appropriate when she felt like it. If we did pinch food – which we did sometimes out of desperation – we were beaten mercilessly in the barn.

One morning, I was enjoying a rare moment of freedom, as Judith had Robert back at George Dowty and I was able to play unfettered for once. Charlotte and I were dressed up in some old ladies' clothes we had found (they must have been John's mother's, I now realize) and were perched on two old rocking horses, swinging wildly back and forth. I was pretending I was a fairy. Then I was a princess or a queen. It was great fun and while I was trying to not make any noise – of course – I was still free to let my imagination soar.

Suddenly, the door flung open and there stood Eunice, dressed in a red outfit, looking very grim. We both stopped rocking immediately and jumped to attention.

'John Drake's dead. Be quiet.'

I don't think we registered what Eunice meant; not at first, anyway. Charlotte and I looked at each other, then back at our horses, and started to rock gently, keen to resume our game, but fearful of angering Eunice.

Then Eunice raised her voice like she meant business. 'I said be quiet. Seriously. He's dead. I'm waiting for the nurse to come.'

Both Charlotte and I stopped rocking and I gingerly climbed off my horse and took off the clothes I'd dressed up in. *Dead. A dead person. In the house.* I wasn't scared – it felt almost cool – although I did feel a bit odd about seeing a dead body. But I also felt a bit sad because although he'd been old and grumpy, John Drake had been a kind person in our lives. After all, he had shared his big house with us.

Eunice, on the other hand, showed no emotion whatsoever. I couldn't tell if she was sad, relieved, happy or even heartbroken. The doctor had visited John the day before and had given him some painkilling drugs. He had been moaning and groaning with pain, but had also been talking quite lucidly about his life before we came. He had slept most of the day, snoring away in his electric chair, but hadn't looked to me like he was about to die. So the idea that he was really gone now was very strange.

Eunice led us in to where John lay in his big reclining chair. I was a bit scared as it looked like John yet, at the same time, not like him. He was all waxy and grey-skinned. His eyes were closed and his mouth was open, sort of slack-jawed. Eunice said to us we didn't need to be afraid of his dead body.

She peered at him, examining his face closely, then said in a loud, flat voice, 'There's nothing there. No more pain now then, John.'

Then Eunice did something really bizarre; it freaked me out. She leant over with her hand and pushed John's jaw up, as if to close it and said in a jolly voice, 'Hello, John, how're you doing?' as if she was playing with a ventriloquist's dummy. Then she started stroking his hands. She said, 'Go on, try it,' and indicated that I should stroke his hand too. I did, briefly. It was ice cold, like marble. Eunice carried on playing with John's dead body as we sneaked out of the room. I paused at the door and looked back, still trying to take in the strange behaviour I'd just witnessed.

Eunice's primary concern was reading the will. She had advised John Drake to make out his will so as not to die intestate, and – surprise, surprise – the farm had been left lock, stock and barrel, to Charlotte, Eunice's favourite. It was to be held in trust until she was eighteen. Eunice had always told John that Charlotte was a good girl and indeed, he had given her a bedroom for herself when we came to live with him, while the rest of us camped on the floor like street urchins. In addition, he had left some money to Eunice.

Eunice had triumphed. She had set her sights on her goal and had attained it. Looking back now, I'm surprised she didn't just sell up George Dowty and bide her time until Charlotte was eighteen and came into her property, as it would have been less to manage. She probably wanted to hold all the property cards to maximize her earnings, like a real-life Monopoly game.

But why did she still need to have all of us kids in tow, costing her money for food, clothes, light and heat? The answer was that Eunice was struggling to keep both properties going, especially in the period before the will had gone through probate, and needed the money she got from fostering.

The next stage of her grand plan, once the money from John came through, was to modernize and renovate the farm as an investment. In the meantime she needed to keep it running and luckily for her she had the help of unpaid domestic labour – in other words, us. Her daughter would keep George Dowty ticking over (Judith was earning money and I'm sure Eunice would have charged her rent to live there) and Eunice would always have that to fall back on if things got too tight financially. Of course, we didn't know any of this at the time.

Now that John Drake was gone and we no longer had to be quiet for him, things began to slide into a punitive mayhem. Instead of being free to be kids and be noisy, we had to be quieter than ever for Eunice: being quiet was being obedient and being obedient meant being honest, true, pure and saved. Thus, Eunice devised even more violent and unspeakably nasty means to make us obey her every whim. She viewed the three of us Bad children – Sarah, Thomas and me – as the lowest of the low. She didn't treat us as human or with any human kindness. We were expensive slaves who had to earn their keep.

By now I had been totally estranged from my parents for some time. The last contact that I had had was when we had gone from George Dowty Drive to visit my parents in their new flat. It had been a tense and awkward visit, with Eunice telling me to be quiet, to call her 'Auntie Eunice' and to behave impeccably.

Since then, all birthday cards and Christmas cards from my parents or Nan to me had been binned unopened. I knew the

Jehovah's Witnesses didn't believe in sending greetings cards as such, but I did wonder why my parents and Nan had forgotten me completely and it made me very sad at times. Had I done something wrong? Did they no longer love me? Or care? Had they forgotten their kid completely?

In fact, Eunice had taken it upon herself to imprison me on the farm, away from George Dowty Drive, without my parents' knowledge or consent. She hadn't adopted me, or Thomas for that matter; she wasn't even our legal foster mum. Yet, she thought she owned us children totally, that we were her property, and that nobody could come between her and her unwilling 'slaves', especially my parents, who were obviously the lowest of the low in her books.

Some changes occurred immediately John Drake died. Eunice now started to keep the curtains closed permanently, so no one could see in from the outside and, of course, we couldn't see out. It did feel like we were imprisoned in some way. Although we now could go upstairs – which was just as dingy and old-fashioned, cluttered and dirty as the downstairs – our living conditions didn't actually improve. There were several cold and damp bedrooms with fusty old beds – enough for each of us to have one – but we all had to sleep in one room together (that is, Thomas, Sarah and I). Charlotte, of course, continued to have her own bedroom, as she still had some privileges over us. Robert also had more privileges and supposedly went in with Eunice, who, of course, had her own room. But in reality, she usually made me look after him so he slept in the same room as the rest of us 'Bad' kids. She just had him with her if she fancied company.

We also had to look after the animals now, so I was given a new chore: feeding and caring for the chickens, who provided us with eggs and meat. I didn't really mind because I'd always loved animals, but it was yet another job I had to do on top of thinking about the shopping and looking after Robert. Eunice went out and bought a variety of breeds because John Drake's chickens were a bit of a motley crew. I remember the white Sultans with their ruffs and feathery feet and the pretty Wyandottes with their lacy markings.

My first job, early in the morning – whatever the weather – was to let the chickens out. I loved the way they went crazy the second I opened the door, cackling and scratching and pushing to get out. And it amused me when I'd see a long line of our geese flying towards the chicken bowl, trying to muscle in on their breakfast. It was always a lively display and something that I felt belonged to me in a funny way. There was so little that was mine that I clung onto anything that was offered.

Indeed, we had some nice breakfasts for a while, with fresh eggs, cereal and toast. We still had to have All-Bran and linseeds, of course, and undergo the daily poo check, but it didn't matter so much, as we had more variety in our diet.

As with all light, however, there is shadow and we were still having our 'proper beaten-style' beatings all the time, including on the soles of the feet, for the smallest things. One day, not long after John had died, I was in the kitchen when Eunice appeared, looking very angry. I was clearly in her Bad Books for some reason.

'Where are those throat sweets I told you to get for Judith?' she demanded.

I knew I was in for it because it was the third day in a row I'd forgotten. There was a little post office down the road where I could have gone to buy them but it had simply gone out of my mind. I knew that saying anything at all would inflame the situation, so I just tried to blank my face and stay still, hoping the storm would pass.

'Cat got your tongue, has it? Well, I'll give you a sore throat, then you'll know how it feels.'

Next, I was being dragged unceremoniously out of the kitchen by my arm and into the living room. Since John had died Eunice had no need to take us out of the house, unless we were out already or she just felt like it, as she could now wield her stick in the comfort of her own home, behind closed curtains. Eunice pointed to the floor so I duly took up my position on my back, took my socks off, rolled up my trouser leg and put one leg in the air. It was always difficult to keep my leg up and I often had to hold it up with both hands, otherwise it wobbled so that she couldn't take aim, prompting yet more punishment.

Eunice brandished her favourite stick – a chair leg, which

she hid in the living room, propped up in a dark corner. She positioned herself alongside my body, as always. But then I noticed there were two sticks this time, not just one.

'Open your mouth.'

What? What's she up to now? I turned my eyes towards her, terrified by what she was going to do now. Coming towards my opened mouth was a long piece of wood, wedge-shaped and about a foot long. To my horror, Eunice thrust the wood into my mouth, past my new front teeth, until it hit the soft tissue at the back of my throat. I retched automatically. It was a natural reaction. Shocked and terrified by what was happening to me, I retched again, tasting the wood. I choked, but couldn't be sick, as I could hardly breathe and was pinned down, flat on my back, like a beetle staked to a tray. In response, Eunice pushed the wood in further. It hurt like hell, and again, I retched involuntarily. I was in complete distress and thought I was going to die. Looking up, past the wood sticking out of my mouth, I could see Eunice's hand clamped firmly on the end, pressing it down into me. On her face was a look of stern concentration. I really thought she was out to kill me; that she might stab me to death through my neck and pin me to the floor. I wriggled to get out from under. I wanted to get away. Fast.

'Stop that. You'll only make it worse for yourself.'

Then I felt the familiar, sickening thwack on the soles of my feet. *Oh no, I'd forgotten all about that – she was still going to beat my feet, too.* I could see the other stick in her right arm being raised over the end of my body. She motioned with her head for me to keep my leg up for her to aim at, so I strained to hold my wobbly leg up to receive the blows. But the pain in the feet somehow didn't count today as my mind was entirely concentrated on trying to breathe with a long piece of hard wood shoved right down into the back of my throat.

Whack. Whack. Whack. Whack. Whack.

Eunice launched a frenzied attack on my feet, but every time I tried to wriggle, scream out or protest, the wedge would be driven further down into my throat and all I could do was gag. I could taste the woody, varnished flavour of the stick, although my tongue was thrust back unnaturally and to the side. It was horrendous. I squirmed, but as I did so, I could feel the double pain of my feet being seared and my throat being pierced from within. *Please make it stop, someone. Please.*

'Relax.'

Relax! Are you crazy? How can I relax?

Eunice stood beside me, her arms out, in a weird crucifix-like stance, legs akimbo, a stick in each hand, as if she was conducting some kind of horrific orchestral piece. But I was the instrument being played, a small, innocent child, supposedly in her care. And what she was conducting was a terrible act of assault. All I had done was forget to buy some throat sweets, and now I was having my throat massacred from within and the soles of my feet destroyed with every lacerating blow.

Afterwards I lay on my side in a foetal position, shaking from the shock, moaning and weeping while holding my throat with both hands. I watched as Eunice put her sticks away in the dark corner with careful precision. I noticed a glint of red on the end of the wedged stick and indeed, my throat felt slashed and raw. I had the metallic taste of blood in my mouth and I lay there, feeling the world had come to an end.

'You won't forget those throat sweets now.' And Eunice swept out of the room to get on with the rest of her day, satisfied with another sadistic, soul-saving job done.

Later, in court, I would hold one of the sticks she routinely used to thrust down our throats and examine the two inches of dried blood staining the end.

CHAPTER 13: *Starvation*

Although I was now about eleven I had never had any pocket money. None of us Bad children did, and therefore we had nothing to spend on ourselves. Of course, we never got paid for any chores we did, like mow the grass or feed the animals, as all of that was to earn our keep.

I know it was wrong, but sometimes we took money from Eunice's purse and sneaked off to the post office to buy sweets or a treat. We didn't mean to be bad, but we were hungry and we were desperate. We knew we were risking terrible punishments, of course, but in a way because we would be beaten for anything as trivial forgetting to buy throat sweets or looking at Eunice in a certain way, it almost felt like we were hung, drawn and quartered before we'd even committed a crime. If I was supposed to be bad, evil and terrible through and through then I might as well be bad, evil and terrible. Anyway, by then, as ghastly as the beatings were, I'd almost become inured to them. That doesn't mean it didn't hurt, but I had found a way to cope with the attacks.

But also, we were moving towards being pubescent teenagers and there was a stirring of hormones in the house. We'd been needy, meek children when she met us, and we'd been brainwashed and beaten into submission for nearly five years. Whether there would ever be an all-out rebellion, where we stood together, locked arms and said 'Enough!' was yet to be seen. But Eunice was very careful to continue to divide and rule all of us, making sure we stayed enemies rather than friends. If we had got together and risen up against her, who knows what the consequences might have been.

Having been maltreated for as long as we had, we began to develop some hardened callouses, not just on our feet, but in our natures, even in our very souls. So, while we knew that stealing money was 'wrong', we also felt *'So what?'* The stick down the throat would be just as horrible whether or not we'd enjoyed some sweeties, so I guess we must have thought it was worth the risk. Of course, I don't think any of this was consciously thought through because when it came down to it we acted quickly and spontaneously, probably desperate for a break from the boredom and monotony of our isolated and peculiar lives on the farm.

John Drake's money finally arrived around now. Not that we were told about it, but Eunice started to enact some of her refurbishment plans at this time, so she must have received some big money from somewhere. This meant there was cash left lying around the house in drawers, sometimes two or three hundred, even a thousand pounds at a time, to pay workmen.

I remember one time an electrician came to do some repairs on the farm's rickety old electrics. Eunice had stashed a large amount of cash in a drawer in the hall to pay him and Charlotte found it and suggested, wildly, that we take some. We were breathless and flushed with the very idea, but we'd learned to keep our faces straight. Years of practice. Amazingly, Eunice was flirting with the electrician – it was so strange to see her being charming and laughing, almost looking attractive and feminine, so completely the opposite of her usual dreary self. So, while Eunice was busy chatting, we helped ourselves to some cash, our hearts in our mouths with a mixture of fear and excitement. I think it was quite a lot, around £200, which was a real fortune to us. Although it was Charlotte's idea, we all joined in because, after all, there was enormous satisfaction in getting one over on Eunice while she was making eyes at the electrician in the kitchen like a total idiot.

We rushed to the post office and had the most fantastic time choosing chocolate bars, chewy sweets and dolly mixtures. It obviously seemed strange to the woman in there that the manky kids from the farm, who never went out, were suddenly loaded. We'd never had so much cash before and it must have seemed very suspicious indeed. Afterwards, triumphant, we ran over the back fields into the bushes behind the farm and gobbled down as many sweets as we could, almost making ourselves sick, while one of us kept a watchful eye out for you-know-who. Eventually, we wandered back home, our tummies full and our tastebuds satisfied. Eunice was waiting for us, po-faced, the flirty smiles all gone.

The woman from the post office had phoned Eunice and told her about us – she was surprised that we'd had so much money and obviously thought Eunice should know. We were in big trouble. This time, in a new twist, Eunice said emphatically it was all my fault. I had turned Charlotte bad, infecting her with my evil. I wasn't one to squeal so Charlotte got let off the beating (she never owned up to the fact it was her idea, of course, to save her own skin) and I took most of the brunt, including a particularly tough session with the wooden wedge rammed down my throat until it bled. Once again my throat was sore for days afterwards, really raspy and swollen, and my feet were black and blue.

In the end, we all learned to switch off emotionally when she beat us and we would end up having surreal conversations with each other, such as, 'We're so lucky 'cos she used the biggest stick on our feet today,' meaning it wasn't as painful as it could have been had she used a smaller stick. The worst was a four-foot bamboo cane, which was so unbearable I couldn't hold out against the stinging agony. I now understand why torturers use bamboo – it certainly does create intense pain. But when Eunice used a broom pole, which was more clunky, that was not so bad. I'm sure she must have got some of her ideas from some Japanese POW memoirs that she once read (hence the bamboo stick). How totally bizarre the world we were living in was: we were actually grateful for being beaten with a broom handle.

Worst of all was when she got us to hold each other down when she was beating us. Sometimes she'd want to concentrate her effort on bashing our feet and needed two hands for the job, so she'd give the wedge over to one of us waiting obediently in the queue to be beaten. This was really warped. Holding the stick in Thomas or Sarah's throat was horribly distressing and is the thing I feel worst about concerning my time at Eunice's. Although I felt I could take her punishment, I didn't want to be party to doling it out to another child because I knew what they would be suffering. I wished at the time that I was big enough to resist, but there was no place for resistance in Eunice's world; we were utterly overpowered at every turn.

After the sweet-stealing incident we were more often in Eunice's Bad Books than her Good Books, which meant more beatings, more punishments and more deprivation. Her mission was to diminish our poor lives further and further and my only weapon was to learn more and more ways to try and endure or outwit her. Sometimes, during beatings, I would bite my hands to stop crying out. Any noise would give

Eunice an incentive to reach for her other stick and ram it down my throat. But there were even tougher testing times ahead, especially as Eunice always prided herself as being one step ahead of us all.

Food increasingly became the battleground between Eunice and us at that time. Even though she probably had more cash now than ever, she reduced our food rations. Thomas, Sarah and myself were obviously not worth feeding properly – at least that was the message we got loud and clear. We were already very skinny, while Charlotte was plump and Robert was growing into a sturdy little boy, so we looked very strange in comparison to each other. However, Eunice was always hovering over the food, counting the slices of bread in the packet, even measuring the Battenburg cake (when we had some, which was rare), to make sure nothing was taken without her knowledge and agreement.

I was supposedly in charge of food, so I was always the first one to be held responsible, although I had no power to dispense it as I saw fair. Not only were our food portions diminishing, but Eunice now began to add starvation to our punishment list.

I must have been about eleven when some food went missing – I can't even remember what it was or how much, but it probably was a slice of bread or a piece of cake or something trivial – and she told me to starve for a day. Now, I was already hungry, having done lots of physical work, like feeding the chickens, watching Robert, cleaning the farm and outbuildings and looking after the dog. I was in the kitchen alone so I opened the bread bin and took out a stale crust and slipped it under my shirt. Then I ran out to the chicken shed, crammed the bread into my mouth and ate it as fast as possible.

It was a freezing cold day, wet and windy outside, and the chickens were restless. I was sweeping up the shed when Eunice appeared at the door, looking angry and sour. 'What have you done?'

I paused from sweeping and tried to make my face blank, hoping there were no crumbs around my mouth. I looked at Eunice, then at the floor. She stared at me, accusingly.

'You've been sly, so you can starve for two days now.'

I opened my mouth to protest, but suddenly thought better of it as that was called 'talking back' and, in itself, was enough to set her off on a beating. Eunice watched my reaction, then turned and left the shed. I had a heavy sense of foreboding. *Starve for two days. Two days!* My mind was racing. I was always hungry. A few hours were OK – I'd missed many meals before – and I could probably even get through a day. But two?

I went back to sweeping, feeling very downhearted, listening to the chickens cluck away contentedly as they pecked the floor. I thought I could eat the chicken feed, or scavenge something out of the pig food. I'd have to be careful though.

Then Eunice appeared again, like a spectre of doom before

me. I jumped. She liked to try to catch me out, catch me at something naughty.

'You'll get a beating. Later. It's a sin to be sly.'

With that she went off, satisfied. Now I felt even worse as not only would I starve, but I'd have to go through a beating, too. And God knows what she had in mind for me this time. I looked out of the shed door at the rain slanting down from the sky and wondered if life would always be like this. Wasn't there any help, anywhere? Who could I tell? Who could help? I'd tried running away, and I'd just been brought back and it had all carried on as before. My life felt hopeless.

Eunice didn't relent, so I did really starve for those two whole days and it was terrible. I also got the beating for being 'sly', into the bargain, the usual soles of the feet routine with a bamboo rod, and I remember beginning to feel so weak that she had to hold my legs up for me so she could beat my feet properly. As I got weaker and weaker, I could hardly walk to the chicken shed – I still had to feed the chickens, if not myself. Not only were my feet battered and bruised, but I was also dragging the heavy hosepipe up to the shed so I could clean it, thinking, *I can't do this.* I know it sounds an absurd situation to be in but I just knew I had to be able to endure anything Eunice threw at me, otherwise I'd simply lie down and die.

Another time, around the same period, a block of cheese went missing from the larder. You'd think someone had stolen the crown jewels from the fuss Eunice made. She was absolutely convinced that I had taken it – and, if not me, it would have been Thomas or Sarah, of course. To this day I think Jet probably took it, as he was always nosing around the kitchen and would gobble up anything in his path, including its cellophane wrapping (he'd simply poo that out again). But because there was no cellophane on the floor or any other obvious evidence, such as crumbs of cheese in his basket, Eunice refused to believe that he was the guilty party. She was always like that – she would survey a crime scene with forensic precision, try to analyse what had happened, then pin it on someone. Of course, she was always convinced from the outset that the main culprits were the three Bad children. So much for innocent until proven guilty.

But with the cheese incident something snapped inside me. I don't know whether I was outraged about being starved, or whether it was the effects of puberty and its associated rebellion, but I had just had enough of it all. I refused to admit that any of us had stolen the cheese – because we hadn't – and for some reason I was totally stubborn over it. I could still be fiery sometimes and while I would usually give in, just to make things easier on us all, this time I couldn't bear to. It seemed so utterly and completely unfair because it wasn't true. Like so many of her crazy accusations. This may have been the beginning of my wanting to fight back in some way, albeit that I still got hurt as a consequence.

Eunice stood there, her arms by her sides, with Thomas, Sarah and myself lined up in front of her. It was like a scene out of *Oliver Twist*. Charlotte hovered around in the background, sniggering, as she frequently did. Robert was in the next room playing. He was often out of the room, or not around, and didn't always see what was going on.

Eunice was staring at us, and at me in particular. 'What have you done with it?'

I hadn't taken the cheese and this time, I wasn't going to take the heat for anyone else. It might be Jet, it might be Thomas or any one of us. I felt stubborn.

'It wasn't me.'

Eunice's stare intensified as she came and bent over me. I could smell her horrible stench – her armpits and breath made me sick.

'Answering back, are we? Well, you can starve.'

I wanted to say, 'Fine!' but I didn't. I knew better than that. I knew when to stop. I just stared back at Eunice, making my eyes dead and blank. She stared back and we were locked together like that for a few moments. Still I wouldn't admit the crime (which I hadn't committed in the first place) of stealing the cheese (a lump of Cheddar, after all).

Eunice seemed annoyed that I wouldn't admit it, but I felt a secret satisfaction at holding out against her. If she wanted me to starve, I could starve. I could do that. I wouldn't buckle.

This was the first moment I had ever really stood up to

her and although it was only a small thing, and I knew I was going to be hungry afterwards, I still felt a tiny edge of triumph. After all, what could she do that was even worse? She could kill me. That would be the next step. And sometimes I thought it would be a happy relief to be dead rather than have to keep on enduring life with Eunice and all her bizarre and cruel rules.

So I starved. But I felt I was starving to prove a point. As each day passed, I continued to refuse to admit to the theft, and she responded with, 'Starve again, then'. I'd think, *OK, you old hateful cow, I'll starve. I'll show you.* It was a real battle of wills and mine was not going to be broken by hers. I was choosing to starve rather than give in and that felt almost powerful.

However, I wasn't pinching any food to survive (she had probably locked all the food up, anyway), so I was really, really hungry. I was so weak and sick I was hallucinating, seeing things that were not there. Finally, desperate to eat something, I resorted to the pig bin and ate pig nuts. They had a bitter, gritty texture, like cardboard. I hated the taste, but just hoped they'd give me some energy to survive. The pigs also had mouldy boiled potatoes, rotten vegetable peel, manky chunks of carrot and cabbage (all the bits we didn't want to eat). I took these and, when Eunice was out or busy elsewhere and I was out of her line of vision and earshot, I quickly boiled them up in a pan in the kitchen and took the unappetizing mess outside, wolfing it down while sitting with the pigs in the sty.

Eventually, maybe after a week, Eunice handed out some food at a mealtime to me, as well as the other children. There was no apology, no explanation, no making up. I was suddenly just included. I guess she felt she had to feed me something or I would die.

So, the rebellion had begun and battle lines had now been drawn. The starvation incident was a major turning point for me as from then on I would try and find other ways of getting round Eunice's punishing edicts.

Eunice still watched us vigilantly, and made us watch and, especially, tell on each other. And since she was now quite busy overseeing the renovations on the farm, she would turn the task of spying over to us more often. So she might command Sarah, 'You watch them and make sure they don't eat anything' (meaning Thomas and me). Sarah would nod meekly and feign total obedience to Eunice, but once she was out of sight, we would pretty much slip each other a slice of bread. As long as we didn't do anything too stupid, we could help each other survive. We had to be careful, though, because Eunice's beady eye would be on us in a trice and any minor gains we made could be snatched away very easily. And she could always make things worse.

Eunice's daily mission seemed to be to make us as miserable as she possibly could by devising more and more unpleasant things for us to eat. If we had anything to eat, that is. For instance, she would delight in ruining something nice for me. On one rare occasion when I actually had a Marmite sandwich all to myself in a quiet moment in the chicken shed (I was probably eating over lunchtime while doing my chores), Eunice came in and claimed I had lied to her about something. I can't even remember what it was now, but it meant that yet again, I was in her Bad Books. She looked at me accusingly, then snatched my sandwich and stooped to wipe it in the chicken poo which was scattered on the floor. Handing me back the sandwich, studded with clumps of chicken poo, she commanded, 'Eat it!' I looked at the sandwich and thought, *No way am I eating that,* but Eunice stood over me and forced me to eat it, every last morsel. It was absolutely disgusting. The poo had stuck to the Marmite and felt and tasted revolting pushed between my teeth. I retched and wanted to be sick, but knew that if I was, she would make me eat that too. I had seen her do that to both Sarah and Thomas before now, and knew how she relished watching them eat something as utterly vile as their own vomit. I managed to keep it down. Just.

As well as the decorating going on around us, Eunice also decided to spend some of her money on throwing a 'Beauty and the Beast' party, a very rare event in our usually isolated household. I don't remember what the point of the party was – I'm not even sure if she ever told us. Eunice ran a small dance class in the village appropriately called (given her high levels of aggression) 'Hopping Mad', and I suppose some of the village people came. I think some Jehovah's Witnesses were invited too, something John Drake would have hated.

I can't really remember exactly who was there but I do remember that for once we had lots of nice food in the house as Eunice had obviously shopped for the party. But the temptation was too great for Sarah and Thomas, who were utterly starving at the time. Recklessly, they stole the Beauty and the Beast theme cake, took it upstairs and ate loads of it. I went up and saw crumbs and icing everywhere and thought, *Oh no, they'll be in for it now.*

Then Eunice appeared with a face like thunder and stood in the doorway. 'Well?' she said. But their crime was obvious, there was no denying it, as only half the huge cake was left on the tray, and there was debris everywhere on the floor and bed. I thought Eunice would tear their heads off with her bare hands, but she went icy cold, which was not a good sign.

Eunice hadn't been feeding them for ages – they were already in her Bad Books – but I was in her Good Books at the time, for some reason. The thing with her punishing regime was when you were in, you were in (fed and not beaten), but if you were out, then you were really out (and starved and beaten). Thomas and Sarah had been so hungry that seeing the party food was just too much for them. Who could blame them, really? The table in the kitchen had been laden with things we never, ever had in the house and the cake looked so delicious it was just too good to be true. They knew they were being naughty, especially after years of living with Eunice and her rules, but their hunger had now placed them beyond reason.

Of course they both got beaten very badly, including the stick-down-the-throat treatment and a foot beating. That went without saying. But then Sarah was made to eat the whole of the rest of the cake. And I was told to watch her and make her do it. It was a massive, rich fruit cake and Sarah had already helped herself to a big portion. She was full but was being forced to eat more and more cake, until she started to throw it back up. Then Eunice made her eat the vomit. Which made her throw up even more, and then she was made to eat that. Then more cake. It was utterly horrendous. Sarah was crying and distressed and I was distraught having to watch her go through this. In the end, while Eunice wasn't looking (for once), and although I was supposed to watch her finish it all, I managed to take the rest of the cursed cake and Sarah's vomit in a bowl and chuck it all over the back of the field, where nobody could see the evidence.

But that wasn't the end of the story. Eunice was convinced that Thomas had taken some chicken nuggets as well. Again, nobody would admit to the crime, even though both Sarah and Thomas were supposed to have been watching each other at the time. This stolen food saga was now reaching epic proportions and I imagined Eunice constructing a gallows on the back lawn. She knew she had to act swiftly and 'teach them a lesson they would never forget'. What followed was so horrific it was, indeed, a lesson none of us would forget. Ever.

Eunice locked both Sarah and Thomas in an upstairs bedroom for a whole month – totally naked – and starved them, with only some water to drink. It was dreadful. She took away their bedding and anything of comfort and a couple of times a day, like a prison warden, she would unlock the door and take them along to the loo and back.

I got very scared thinking about what was going on in there and at night I would lie awake on my cushion on the floor and listen out. It was horribly quiet. I wanted to take them some food up, but Eunice sensed I would and was more vigilant than ever, doling out the food herself and keeping a tight rein on everything in the kitchen. She would push the occasional sandwich under the door for them, but this was not much for two starving children.

One day I heard Eunice's voice raised and I crept upstairs. The door was open and I could see in to where she was standing, legs apart, hands on hips. Beyond her, I could see Thomas's face, pale and thin. Then Eunice pointed to something on the floor – a puddle where Thomas had urinated out of desperation. She made him kneel down and lap up the urine, like a dog. I heard afterwards that Sarah had done a poo in the room and had hidden it under one of the loose floorboards. But at other times she was forced to eat her poo, as was Thomas. It was worse than any punishment I had thought Eunice capable of creating. I remembered having my face pushed into Jet's poo and Robert's nappy, so I knew a bit about how revolting that could be. But to eat it?

But worse – if I'm honest, I was just glad it wasn't me up there and that made me feel horribly guilty. Eunice did lock me in the room at one point for half an hour to 'teach me a lesson' for something and it was appalling to see how they were living. It was a total unsanitary mess and I couldn't wait to get out of there. Thomas and Sarah were thin and pale and very shocked at what was happening to them. They just lay prone and naked on the floorboards, not moving or saying anything, waiting passively for time to pass. They really were starving to death. It was without doubt the worst, most terrifying punishment any of us had ever had.

I wondered if she'd really let them die of starvation and what *I* would do if it went that far. I think she did want to kill us, the lowest of the low in her mind. This month of punishment made us all feel that Eunice could do absolutely anything she wanted with us, even destroy us. She had us totally in her power.

Although I wasn't locked in the room with the other two, I wasn't to escape Eunice's daily punishing whims. I might have started off this period in her Good Books, but at some point during that very gloomy time, I descended into her Bad Books, with horrible consequences.

One morning, I went to make breakfast and there she was, by the counter in the kitchen, looking incandescent. She was holding up the porridge oats bag and looking at me with her piercing gaze.

'What's this?'

I felt like saying, 'A porridge oats bag', but I knew better. There was obviously something seriously wrong.

'You left it out.'

Eunice tipped the contents of the bag onto the side and the oats spilled out. I could see little brown lumps in the mixture: mouse or even rat droppings. There had been some rats around the garden recently and the outbuildings, as the farm was falling into terrible disrepair – since John Drake had died there was rubbish and clutter everywhere. I had obviously left the porridge bag out after using it the day before and some droppings had got into the bag.

Eunice said nothing more, but scraped the oats off the side and put them into a saucepan, poo and all. She then poured in some water, and stirred.

'I'll make your breakfast for you.'

I looked on horrified as she stirred the gooey mix on the stove. Her back was to me as I stood behind her in the kitchen and I tried to think of all the different things I could do to escape. I could faint, run out of the room, take it and then bin it or throw it over the hedge, as I had done with the rest of Sarah's cake vomit. Eunice continued stirring very calmly. As ever, she was a woman on a mission. When the 'porridge' was cooked, she spooned a large, steaming helping into a bowl. It was a bigger portion than she would usually allow me for breakfast. This was obviously a special 'treat'.

'Sit down.'

I sat down slowly at the table.

She handed me a spoon. 'Eat it.'

When I didn't move, Eunice pushed the spoon into the bowl and brought out a stinking, heaped spoonful and waved it in front of my mouth. The smell wafted up my nose and I felt my stomach churn. She pushed the spoon against my closed lips. 'Open wide.'

I knew better than to try to resist, so I opened my mouth and took the vile mixture, wanting to retch at the first mouthful. It tasted like the soles of my wellingtons after I'd cleaned out the chicken shed. My gorge rose and I could see a glint in Eunice's eyes – her satisfaction would be complete if I threw up there and then.

I blanked out, using my technique of turning myself off at the emotional mains and I ate the whole lot. I could tell Eunice was waiting for me to give up, so she could administer my next beating, but I was determined to show her what I was made of.

'Have you held it down?'

She was watching me like a hawk, hoping against hope that I would spew. Again, this was a battle of wills and I was not going to be beaten. She wanted to hurt me, but I was not going to give her the satisfaction of thinking I cared. I had stood up to her before and starved for days, now I could eat this. I would win.

'Yeah,' was all I could manage through a constricted throat. I just had to stop myself thinking about those rat or mice droppings mingled in with the oats, which were now sitting, like a smouldering rock, in my stomach.

She was disappointed, clearly, that I was managing to keep down her vile concoction. Eunice liked nothing more than to reduce me to jelly and I was not going to comply. Something in me needed to show her that I was her match. She didn't quite know how to handle the situation now that I hadn't crumbled.

'Well, you do that again and you'll get it again.'

I have to hold it down now. Just blank yourself out.

Eunice started tidying up and I feigned as much nonchalance as I could muster while my stomach heaved. I stood up and pushed back my chair, the kitchen table reeling in front of me. I could still feel my gorge rising, but I swallowed hard as saliva filled my mouth and kept my face as blank as I could. I moved towards the door, slowly, and walked a few steps across the yard, trying to be as cool as a cucumber.

Once out of her sight, I ran like the clappers down the field.

When a May bug flew into my hair it brought me back to myself, and now that I was beyond the kitchen and Eunice's evil gaze I could allow my feelings back into my body and brain. I was more scared of the May bug than I was of the ghastly porridgy mess that was sloshing around in my guts. Finally, at the edge of the field I threw up the entire contents of my poisoned stomach. What a relief. There was some minor satisfaction in having triumphed over Eunice and having ruined her quest to reduce me to a blubbering wreck. I chalked one up to me in the increasingly tough war of wills between us.

The Home Tutor Inspector would still pay us occasional visits, but there would always be a written warning, so we'd be driven back to George Dowty Drive, all scrubbed up and the house would be hurriedly tidied. Eunice would buy some new books, as usual, and we would pose, as if we were working away merrily every day, happily fed by a loving 'mummy'. Afterwards we'd be whisked back to our enslaved drudgery at the farm, which got grimmer and grimmer by the month.

The farmhouse must have looked so odd from the outside, with the curtains permanently drawn and five unnaturally quiet children moping about, dressed in rags, three of them seemingly half-starved. I remember the local vicar came round and dared to ring the doorbell once and my little heart scampered with hope as I silently prayed, *'Please, please, save us.'* But Eunice only opened the front door a tiny crack and told him, in no uncertain terms, 'We're all Jehovah's Witnesses here,' sending him firmly away with a giant flea in his ear. As far as I know, he never returned but he did write to social services.

I heard at the trial that somebody had even told social services about our washing-up liquid treatment – goodness knows how that had got out – and still no one rescued us.

CHAPTER 14: *Growing Pains*

I had now started to 'develop' into a young woman, but Eunice had not provided me with any sex education whatsoever as part of her so-called 'home tutoring' service. As I was never allowed to read novels, magazines, newspapers or watch educational TV, I had no means of finding things out for myself. If anything, we had been given an immense amount of misinformation, and a lot of fear about sex, bodies and relationships.

Although I looked after the chickens and helped to breed them, I still didn't understand much about reproduction. I remember thinking that the cockerel must mount the hen and somehow squirt juice into her neck. I had picked up the term 'mount' from Eunice, without understanding the reality of what the chickens got up to in the back of the shed. Even at eleven going on twelve, I was still confused about how the hen's egg got fertilized, as I knew nothing at all about human reproduction. So kissing, petting, pregnancy – all of those – were completely foreign territory. Even when I came across sex – in all its various forms – as I got older, I still didn't know what to expect. But while I was very ignorant indeed, I was obviously curious, like any normal, growing child.

Eunice never took us to the doctor or dentist. Even when I got pecked by a chicken and the cut got infected, she didn't bother taking me to the doctor. If it was a real emergency and she had to take us for treatment, she made sure she did all the talking for us. We were never allowed to offer an opinion and were threatened before we went in. I guess she was scared we'd give the game away. No dentist ever picked up on the fact that Sarah's bashed-in front teeth were due to Eunice's maltreatment. She'd had to go to the dentist several times and must have looked shut-down, skinny and strange. But it seemed to me that doctors and dentists always believed the adults rather than the children, or didn't really use their eyes or intuition in any way.

On one particular occasion we were all at the dentist because Thomas had a toothache. I went to the loo and found blood in my pants. I was terrified. What was going on? What on earth had happened?

Eunice was sitting in the waiting room, flicking through a women's magazine (I'm not sure this was allowed by the Jehovah's Witnesses). Robert was sitting next to her, playing with a toy and Charlotte was sitting on her other side. I looked at Eunice, who carried on reading. I stood in front of her and whispered, hoping no one else would hear, 'I'm dying, I've started bleeding – something's wrong.'

Eunice continued to read for a moment. Then she folded the magazine and looked up at me, expressionless. I was scared, and the other kids were listening, so it was embarrassing, too.

'You will start bleeding. It's your age. It'll happen every month, like clockwork.'

Every month from now on? But why? I had no idea. Was it an illness?

Robert had lost interest in the toy and had wandered over to look at the fish tank, so I took his seat next to Eunice. She had gone back to looking at the magazine, obviously thinking the conversation was over.

'Why?'

Eunice looked up at me, clearly bored by the whole business. 'Inside you've got a womb and it's expelling badness from your body. You've got bad blood, and your womb expels that evil blood from you to cleanse your soul.'

Ah, of course. That made complete sense. I felt a bit shocked that I would have to live with this from now on. I must be really bad inside and I imagined this pit of bloody badness oozing out of me into my knickers every month, like a disease.

Eunice turned away again and went back to reading, satisfied she'd explained everything to me clearly.

I didn't question her explanation. How could I? I'd been brainwashed for over five years to believe the worst of myself all the time. So my menstruation was yet another sign of how evil and bad I was. It definitely all made sense. Nevertheless the whole business took a bit of getting used to, especially as I got no 'motherly' sympathy when I got my monthly tummy cramps.

My body was beginning to change, too, as I began to grow hair under my armpits and 'down there', my hair got greasier and my breasts began to develop. Again, there was no gentle guidance or help in understanding what was happening to me. There was no going out to buy my first bra with my mum. I had a ropy, old, greyish-white hand-me-down from a charity shop, which was way too big. As usual, I was made to feel I just wasn't worth any fuss.

Although we almost never had visitors to the farmhouse Eunice did have an old friend – I'm going to call him Kevin, although that's not his real name – who popped in very occasionally for a cup of tea. She told us to call him 'Uncle' although he wasn't related. I don't know where she knew him from but he was quite a rough type. He was a very odd-looking guy and uncomfortably physical, always insisting that we sat on his lap. Or rather, me, to whom he had taken a particular fancy.

Kevin seemed very interested in my developing body. I would sit on his lap and he would put his arms around me. Then he would put his hands on my legs and move them up my thighs. One day, he put his hands on my crotch and began to rub me, which felt very peculiar and I didn't know what I should do. I couldn't run away as he held me tightly there, on his lap. I just sat there, passively, as he rubbed me between the legs, breathing heavily. I was really embarrassed, and also confused, because I didn't understand what exactly was going on.

On another occasion, he started asking me strange questions. 'How are you down there? Are you hairy or bald?'

I didn't know how to answer him, it felt so rude and personal, but I felt I had to obey, so I said, 'I've got some hair.'

Kevin then became very interested and started leering at me, saying, 'You know, you're a very attractive girl,' which freaked me out. I fought to get off his lap and, after quite a struggle, I did. However, every time he visited he was always hanging around me, trying to touch my body, especially my private parts, and I absolutely hated it.

Another time when he dropped in unexpectedly, Kevin got me on his lap again and was rubbing me 'down there'. Then he told me to touch his trousers in the crotch area. He said, 'Go on, touch it'. But I didn't want to. It didn't feel right at all to do what he wanted. The way he was looking at me made me feel very uncomfortable, as all the while he tried to rub me between my legs. He then said, 'I'll give you a quid if you touch it.' By 'it' I sort of guessed he meant his thing, as I'd seen my foster brother naked and knew men were different 'down there'. I had an idea of what he was getting at, although I didn't really know anything about sex then. I wouldn't have known about men getting erections or ejaculation.

I didn't feel right about what was going on between us but I suppose, on some strange level, Kevin provided human contact, some kind of touch and warped affection, even though it made me feel like I wanted to curl up into a ball of embarrassment and shame. Anyway, I didn't know who I could tell about it, or if anyone could stop him. I certainly didn't think of telling Eunice because I was always in the wrong, before I'd even tried to explain something. She would blame me, tell me I had led him on.

So every time Kevin dropped in he would make a beeline straight for me, and keep trying to get me on his lap to touch me whenever he could. What's more, it got worse and worse the older and more developed I became.

Kevin's behaviour wasn't the only thing that confused me about sex. Eunice had continued to show us horrible things on video or TV, like *The Birds*, when she wanted to 'teach us a lesson'. Around this time she forced me to watch an episode of *Bad Girls* – a late-night drama series on TV for adults about women in prison. I hadn't watched it before, or anything like it, and didn't know the characters or the storyline. Anyway, the one episode Eunice made me watch showed a gang of women prisoners basically raping another woman in the prison. It was horrendous. I saw her being beaten up as they called her names and pulled her hair and boobs.

Eunice turned to me and said, 'That's how you'll end up. You'll end up in prison, just like her.'

It did traumatize me as I felt she was telling me I'd be raped and hurt because I deserved it. I didn't know women did that kind of thing to each other. And I didn't like the idea of ending up in prison either, but Eunice obviously thought I was so evil that that was going to be my future career path. In fact, Eunice had often used that kind of threat before, saying we'd all be taken away by social services if we didn't do what she wanted. Coercion and threats were the name of her daily game. Ironically, it would have been a blessing for us if we had been taken away by the authorities.

Occasionally, Eunice would make us do something which, compared to everything else she put us through, probably seems relatively benign, yet it still makes my stomach churn to think about it. She would make us massage her, as though we were her pampering slaves. She would lie on the floor or on a sofa and read a women's magazine and we would have to massage her feet and her back. It was revolting to have to touch and give pleasure to this woman who hurt us so much. Also, I found her physically disgusting and as I was being told to pick the dead skin off her flat feet, or massage her bony shoulders, I would look with fascination at her saggy boobs hanging around her armpits, or her dry wrinkly skin. Afterwards we would laugh about it together and mimic her, albeit very quietly. These were among the few rare moments when we were able to be united against her in revulsion. It was also one of the few times I can remember when Charlotte didn't grass on the rest of us.

Other than this, we were still supposed to be doing our daily schoolwork, on top of running the farm while Eunice renovated it, but we often got behind in what she set us to do. I never felt like doing any schoolwork, but I'd be beaten if I didn't. I would also be set to make the other children do their work, and if they didn't, we'd all be beaten and forced to stay up all night and do it. I remember having to do a hundred pages of 'I must do my schoolwork' lines and not being allowed to go to bed before I'd done them. It took most of the night to do it. I was utterly exhausted in the morning.

Thomas also got lines for not doing his schoolwork, and I remember helping him as he was a slow writer. I used to let him go to sleep while I did it for him, copying his handwriting, and then I'd wake him up if Eunice was coming so he could pretend he'd been doing them. I sometimes felt protective towards him, although I did get angry with him; but it was easier for me to do it than for him to spend hours and hours trying to finish it.

This kind of thing was a regular occurrence, which was madness as we were already tired and hungry all the time. I was doing all the cooking by then, even making roast dinners or curries and rice, keeping the house tidy, cleaning up, looking after the chickens, Jet and the two black pot-bellied pigs Bunty and Bessie.

Eunice just let the place go, I'm not sure why. Was she lazy, or disorganized? Perhaps she was naturally untidy, or perhaps it was because she was an obsessive hoarder. I remember that George Dowty was full of old dingy toys going back to her own girls' childhoods, as she never threw a single thing away. If a teacup broke, she wouldn't mend it, but would keep the pieces for ages. I was supposed to tidy up, but it was almost impossible, because of the mess we were constantly living in. Yet, if I didn't do a good job, Eunice would confiscate something of mine, like a favourite toy, so I was in a double bind all the time, and actually being sabotaged by Eunice herself.

Although she was a slob, Eunice would come into the kitchen and do a sudden 'spot check', running her fingers over the surfaces for inspection, like a military matron.

Eunice was also fanatical about not putting food in the bin. It was not allowed. So if any food was left over, it had to go back into the fridge, where it would go mouldy. But when this happened it was somehow our fault and we still had to eat it. If we didn't, we got into trouble and were punished.

Because Eunice was still starving us on and off, she was more keen than ever on her 'spot checks' to measure the food in the kitchen. We were growing, hungry children but we were all only still allowed four slices of white bread a day, the cheapest, nastiest brand, sometimes with Heinz sandwich spread on it. We were only ever allowed fruit if we were in her Good Books, and then only one piece each after dinner. I never could have asked her to buy some, or asked for money to go and get some from the shop. In fact, I was never able to ask her for anything at all.

One day, Eunice came into the kitchen and went straight over to the bread bin and threw it open. There was some bread missing – she was convinced – and there would be hell to pay. Eunice grabbed me, pushed up my sleeve and marched me over to the Raeburn, which was burning hot. She lifted up the large cast-iron lid and I could feel the searing heat of the hotplate hit my face in a blast. Eunice had my arm firmly in her claws.

'I can't abide lying. "Thou shalt not steal" is one of the Ten Commandments.'

And with that she pulled my arm roughly and positioned my hand, palm down, about an inch from the burning surface of the hotplate. My reaction was to pull back from the heat, which I could feel was going to blister me. I tried to wriggle away but Eunice held me fast.

'Own up. Who was it?'

It wasn't me. I hadn't touched the bread. I was trying to pull away from the heat, now searing into my hand, but Eunice kept hold of me, hurting my wrist in her strong grasp, and dragging my hand even lower. I was sure I was going to start frying. Behind me the other children stood silently afraid, watching the spectacle, and I could feel their eyes boring into my back, but even so, the culprit, who was in the kitchen, didn't own up. My hand, meanwhile, felt like it was starting to melt and I didn't know if I could stand much more.

'You know what happens to liars? It's like this in the flames of hell, their tongues melt, their eyes melt, their skin falls off their bodies, and they are in unbelievable pain . . .'

Eunice was off on one of her hellfire speeches and meanwhile my hand was sizzling in her scrawny grasp. It was all too much, and the real thief was clearly not going to own up and save my skin.

'It was me.'

'The demons in you know no bounds.'

Just when I felt I couldn't bear another second Eunice released me, satisfied she had flushed out the wicked demon, yet again. Of course I was guilty. I was evil all the way through. My soul would be saved, although my body would be sorely abused. I rushed to the sink to thrust my throbbing hand under running cold water as tears stung my eyes. I blinked back the tears, determined not to show Eunice that she'd hurt me in any way. I was shaking with fear and pain, but again, I tried to hide the tremors from her beady gaze.

As if all this wasn't enough, Eunice had also devised yet another nasty punishment. She must have lain awake at night thinking of what horrible things she could do to us next to 'teach us a lesson'. She developed a new form of torture called the 'invisible chair'. We had to crouch down on our haunches in a sitting position, with our backs or shoulders leaning against the wall, sort of squatting, and we'd have to stay there for ten minutes to an hour, maybe even two. I found it difficult to stay upright, and my legs ached terribly, so I'd often fall over, but Eunice would watch and hit me with a stick, or shout that I had to get back into the upright, crouching position in the invisible chair and stay there until she was satisfied.

She'd make us do this for all sorts of reasons, sometimes very petty ones. One time, I turned on the TV without permission and watched some ice-skating, I think it was Torvill and Dean and it looked magical. But Eunice caught me and I was made to go in the invisible chair by the wall for two hours.

Eunice had occasionally done this kind of thing before. Back in George Dowty Drive, when I still had long hair, she had tied my ponytail to the door handle to stop me falling over. I thought it was less painful having my hair pulled than having to crouch in the semi-sitting position, although neither was particularly pleasant to endure, especially both at the same time.

I was so scared of Eunice that one time when I lost the key to the chicken shed I simply hadn't the nerve to tell her. I was so terrified of what she might do to me that I lied. I told her that there had been a man in the chicken shed trying to steal them and that I'd opened the door and caught him red-handed, but I had run away, dropping the key as I went. It was quite a story (I had a good imagination and was convincing) and she believed it. She marched out to the shed but couldn't find the key in the dark. However, she was clearly spooked about someone coming onto the farm, and I even had a rare card from Eunice saying how brave I was to stand up to the bird snatcher.

After that Eunice called in her first ex-husband and asked him to come and guard the chickens with her for the next three months. The poor man had to sleep in the old rickety caravan in the farmyard. However, he still worshipped her – God knows why – and was happy to come and help her the minute she called him. I felt bad about getting the poor man involved, especially when there was no one in the shed in the first place. But my fear of Eunice had led me to lie, which was ironic, as she was always convinced I was lying anyway.

One Christmas, the chickens really were stolen, though. It made me feel better about lying as it really did happen in the end, but I was upset as I had felt they were my friends, and now I was left with only two chickens, Lady and Queenie (I'd given them all names by then) and some cockerels who – without their usual female companions to occupy them – spent their time fighting. The burglary made me feel spooked myself, especially as I think the thieves had scouted around our farm the day before, asking about a derelict car, a Scimitar, that we now had in the farmyard. They asked me all about the chickens, whether they were good layers or not, and then the next day they were all gone apart from two.

It had never occurred to me to ask those men for help to escape, or to tell them what was going on with Eunice. I had been trained to pretend that everything was fine whenever I came into contact with anyone in the outside world. I was also too terrified of blowing the whistle on Eunice because of the range of terrible punishments which would inevitably come my way as a consequence. She was the all-seeing, all-knowing controller of our little, meaningless lives.

CHAPTER 15: *Any Means of Escape*

I've never really been sure why Eunice took on five children after her two daughters had grown up but, as I mentioned earlier, I'm sure part of the reason was that she saw us as a meal ticket. She was already claiming allowances for both 'fostering' and 'home tutoring', but another way of gaining money from playing the system was to have us registered as disabled in some way. So at different times Eunice campaigned to get Sarah, Thomas and myself – who she believed behaved badly anyway – diagnosed as being on the autistic spectrum. She would then be eligible for disability carer's allowance for each child if she succeeded.

Somehow or other Eunice had got a prescription for Ritalin for Sarah. I think she had taken her to a specialist at some point earlier and had her diagnosed as autistic. In my opinion, Sarah was probably just totally traumatized by years of enduring Eunice's appalling regime, especially after the horrific month of being locked up and starved. Rather than being autistic she was shut down with shock and fear after so much abuse and negligence. Or she may have been depressed and sad as several people noticed later, such as the Jehovah's Witnesses she made friends with. However, at this time Eunice succeeded in getting the diagnosis she wanted and having found that a relatively easy process she then tried the same strategy with Thomas. He was apparently diagnosed with ADHD (Attention Deficit Hyperactivity Disorder) and was prescribed Ritalin too. Later she would do the same for Robert, who really *was* quite hyperactive – and I should know, as the person who looked after him most of the time.

But Eunice had another, even more sinister, motive for getting hold of the tablets. She believed that at Armageddon soldiers would come and put to the sword anyone who wasn't a true believer in her religion. The 144,000 that would be saved would go to heaven, and the rest of us lesser mortals would die a horrible, painful death of the most unbelievably gruesome kind. Eunice told us she was hoarding tablets to take when the soldiers came to get us. We would have to commit mass suicide if we didn't want to be killed by them. She would ram her theory into us over and over. The upshot was that Eunice hoarded drugs in the house, although she also used them to keep us children quiet.

So it was only a matter of time before Eunice decided, when I was about twelve, that I was the next suitable candidate for 'treatment'. I remember being taken to see a psychologist. She may have been the same one Sarah and Thomas had been taken to earlier, or maybe Eunice was working her way through different doctors to avoid being found out. Before I went into the room to meet the doctor, Eunice primed me on how I was to behave, on pain of punishment, of course, if I didn't comply. I had to pose as if I had Asperger's. She had done her research and explained I had to be very inarticulate and shut down. Eunice made it very clear that I had to say absolutely nothing if I was spoken to, and not reply if I was asked a question directly. I had to keep my head down, look at the floor and she would do all the talking. The routine was to be similar to that of our rare visits to the doctor or dentist.

On this occasion, however, the psychologist smelled a rat. I was asked questions, and I kept my eyes down, staring at the carpet, not answering, like I'd been told to, while Eunice talked about how difficult I was to get through to, how shut down I was, and so on. For some reason, and I don't know why, the psychologist did not buy into the Asperger's stunt and sent us home without a prescription. As I left her office she said, 'I think you're playing games with me,' and I had to fight to keep my composure as I wanted to crack up laughing. Maybe she knew I was acting, I don't know.

I found out later, when I was preparing for the court case, that the psychologist had written a report saying I was depressed – well, who wouldn't have been depressed, living with Eunice? – but nothing was ever done about it. I don't know whether this was conveyed to Eunice or not.

Anyway, Eunice was utterly furious that I hadn't convinced the psychologist and told me I would be dealt with the minute we got back to the farm, so the journey home was full of doom, gloom and dread. Journeys home were often like that, heavy, under threat. Once home, and after a thorough beating, Eunice decided to see for herself if I had Asperger's or not. So she gave me some of the other children's prescriptions of Ritalin for a week to 'sort me out'. To my mind now, from an adult perspective, and as a mum, I feel this was not only incredibly dangerous (to give me drugs prescribed for somebody else) but also evil and utterly irresponsible because, in doing so, Eunice set me off in a direction which, until then, I didn't know existed.

I basically got hooked on the drugs straight away because their effect brought me complete psychological relief from all the isolation, fear and pain that I was experiencing daily. I knew where the supply of drugs was because Eunice had put me in charge of administering them to the other children so I began to administer them to myself as well. I began to use them at night, taking up to ten or twelve tablets. Later I'd be taking about fourteen or sixteen tablets a night. Of course now I realize this was fantastically dangerous.

So there I would be, all warm and cosy, wrapped in my blankets and I'd take the tablets. Then a strange thing would happen. I'd start speeding, rushing, but I'd be watching the clock and it would seem to be going very slowly indeed. I'd think, *Ooh, I've got another three hours snuggled up*. My head would be buzzing away but the more I looked at the clock, the slower it would become.

While I was taking the drugs, I also experienced hallucinations, and sometimes I'd 'see' Eunice shouting at me to get up. Then I'd realize it wasn't her; it was my mind playing tricks. Other times I'd envisage cats coming up to me and I'd go to stroke them, then I'd think, *Oh, they're not there*. I'd realize then it was the drugs, like a kind of psychedelic trip. It was really weird.

I know that taking the tablets was wrong, but at the time they provided me with a means of escape. I could remove myself from the horrible world I was forced to live in, with its constant punishments, beatings and rigid rules, and I could snuggle down and disappear into my whizzing mindscape. Best of all was the way they made the night seem so long, rather than just feeling like it lasted for five minutes. Because I was so tired all the time, and daytime on the farm was so foul, it often felt like I just had five minutes to myself – just five minutes of not being watched, punished or having to work, before I went to sleep, then five minutes before I got up and was back in the world of responsibilities and beatings. I could never sleep in, or relax, or enjoy myself.

We weren't allowed any music or the radio, but as I moved into my teens, I would sneak under my covers a mini-radio I found on the farm, and listen secretly all cosy, my mind racing and staring at the clock. I would listen to the music thinking, *Oooh, this is rude,* or *Wa-hey, this is cool,* and feel like a real growing teenager. I couldn't dance around my bedroom as the music was 'too sexual' and corrupting so all I had to relieve my isolation and boredom was a sneaky listen to Shania Twain and the comfort of a 'high' induced by the stolen Ritalin.

Eunice had hoarded so many pills over the years – I guess she kept getting repeat prescriptions – that she didn't notice her stash was going down. So I continued to take Ritalin for a very long time, probably three years or more, tripping the night away – at least, on the nights I was allowed to go to bed.

One of my regular duties was to make Eunice a hot-water bottle at night (another feature of being her slave) and sometimes it would leak into her bed. It actually wasn't my fault – the hot-water bottle was an old one, and it might have been the seams giving way. However, Eunice's predictable response was to make me stand up all night, naked, at the end of her bed. She said I had made her cold and wet, so she would make me cold all night. This was very embarrassing for me because I was now extremely self-conscious about her looking at my developed body. She would fall asleep, of course, and I would want to cover up, sit down or lie down. I'd even doze off and find myself curled up on the floor, but then she'd wake up every so often and shake me, or shout at me, and I had to spring back to my standing position. Naked. At the end of her bed. All night. Then I was supposed to do my full day's duties after this, including schoolwork.

Several times Eunice made me go out into the garden, completely naked, at three in the morning. She even did this at George Dowty Drive somewhat later, when there were teenage boys next door. It was an absolutely humiliating punishment and, having become a typical self-conscious teenager, I felt utterly horrified that one of the boys might see me over the fence.

I have no idea why Eunice did this kind of thing. Overall, she had a very strange and confused attitude to nakedness, in that she would say it was natural and fine for us children to be naked, but she was also very prudish about anything to do with sex or sexuality.

Eunice devised another punishment involving nakedness in which she would stand me in a bath and pour water over my face so I couldn't breathe. She would yank my head back, usually by the hair, and pour a jug of cold water over my face. I always struggled and spluttered when she did something like this – I couldn't help it. Then she would snap, 'Relax, you can breathe,' at me, but I just couldn't. I'd be terrified, panicking, and anyway how could I relax when I was freezing cold, totally naked and was having icy water poured continuously over my face?

The other way Eunice liked to do her 'water torture' was to

fill the bath, then make me kneel beside it so she could dunk my head in and hold it under. I knew she'd read *A Child Called It* by David Pelzer, in which he described the terrible abuse he suffered as a child. His horrible mother did something similar, making him lie in a bath filled with cold water. Who knows whether Eunice 'borrowed' some twisted ideas about child cruelty from that book? She even suggested we read it one time, to show us what happened to bad children.

Because the Raeburn was often slow to warm up the bath water Eunice would often run a bath for Robert, then test the temperature. Sometimes she even dunked my head in to test it and if it was cold, or too cold for Robert, I had to have a cold bath. Nowadays I can't abide cold water; I can never get into a cold bath or swimming pool, even on a warm summer holiday – the memory of being dunked in all that cold water has simply never gone away.

By the time I was thirteen I was way behind with my homework. Eunice was a bad teacher and I didn't want to learn from her. None of us children really did much work, but we were always made to feel we were bad as we were always terribly behind. One time the Home Tutor Inspector was due the next day and Eunice wanted to show him that she had taught the children in her care well. She looked at our books with disgust, then set us all to fill our workbooks with essays and drawings, giving us loads of maths homework to do as well. It was about three times as much work as we normally had, and although I tried I didn't manage to get mine finished in time, what with all the housework, childcare and animal feeding I had to do as well. When Eunice found out she went horribly quiet, which meant I was in big trouble.

'You'll stay up all night until it's finished. Then I'll teach you a lesson.'

I said nothing, but looked down at the homework books on the table. Eunice glared at me and I could tell she was beside herself with anger because she was so steely.

'You can rest assured I'll beat you and beat you, black and blue until you've done it all.'

Eunice went out and left me sitting at the table piled high with books. I was being starved at the time, so I felt hungry, weak and tired even before I started. It was midwinter, freezing cold (it was always cold in the farmhouse, but it seemed colder and bleaker than ever that night), and I stayed up, poring helplessly over my books. Everything swam before my eyes and I couldn't seem to make any sense of what I was supposed to do. I began to panic. I couldn't bear the pressure of knowing how Eunice would react if I hadn't finished by the morning. It would be torture, I was sure. Thomas had also been set a night of homework, but he was already slumped over his books, fast asleep. I didn't have the heart to wake him up, although I knew he'd be in for it, too, if he didn't finish. It all seemed completely hopeless.

As the cold light of dawn approached I began to really panic. It was a similar feeling to the time when I'd run away and hid under the car and in the donkey shed. I just wanted to escape from this terrible, oppressive place. As I looked around the cluttered, dirty room, and saw the pile of un-done homework in front of me, I just couldn't cope. I jumped up and went downstairs to the kitchen. I knew where Eunice kept her private stash of chocolate and I got it out, my heart pounding in my chest. I ate a couple of squares and was blown away by the wonderful sweet taste as they melted in my mouth. Desperate for food and pleasure, I greedily ate the lot, then found another bar and ate that too. Eunice would go berserk once she found it missing, but I suddenly didn't care.

Against her explicit wishes, I found a pop video and slipped it into the TV in the living room. I turned the sound down quite low, so I wouldn't wake her up – it was still very early, only about five in the morning. Then I wrapped myself up in a blanket and watched the video. I loved every minute of it, wowed by the music and the beat, scoffing more chocolate as I watched. Then, realizing it was nearly morning, I got terribly scared. What would Eunice do if I hadn't done the homework? What would happen if she found I'd eaten the chocolate and watched TV without her permission? I'd eaten so much chocolate I felt sick, but it was also wonderful to have a full tummy for once.

I suddenly knew what to do, how to get away from the

constant fear and punishments. I rushed to find the Ritalin pills in Eunice's hoarding place. There were several bottles there, unopened, and I guzzled as many tablets as I could with gulps of water. I kept taking them and taking them, stuffing them into my mouth; I might have taken about thirty altogether. I began to feel woozy as I went back to the TV and wrapped myself up again in the blanket. As my head began to float to the ceiling, I watched the TV melt sideways into a weird shape and suddenly felt happy. Nothing could get me now. I could drift away to nowhere, and it would all be over.

Some time later I saw Eunice's face hovering just above mine, looking stern and intense. My legs were twitching, but I couldn't really feel them. I felt like I was underwater, swimming in a deep, dark ocean; I'd float up to the surface occasionally and then dive back down. My body was jumping around but I couldn't feel it at all. Eunice's face disappeared into a black space. I think I was only semi-conscious, drifting back and then away again just as fast. I have flashes of being in Eunice's car while Judith held me up – they were taking me to the hospital I later realized – before it all went blank.

I finally came to and became gradually aware of Eunice sitting by my side in her grey outfit, looking very emotionless. I couldn't work out where I was or what had happened for a moment. I just felt empty. Eunice said nothing when she noticed I was awake and I just lay there, numb and exhausted. Then she leant forward and said, 'You were fitting'.

I couldn't work out what she meant at first and looked at her blankly.

'You were having a fit. But they pumped your stomach, so you'll live.'

It all came rushing back: the homework, then the chocolate, the video, the pills. Eunice knew. I must be in hospital. I was still alive.

Eunice leant forward and put her hand on top of mine. She started stroking it gently. I was almost shocked, as this was so unusual for Eunice. What did she want?

'You know I love you, don't you?'

I blinked confusedly, trying to take it all in. I felt very thirsty now, sick and my throat was sore. My stomach and head hurt.

'I've only ever wanted what's best for you. I've tried to improve you. But I do love you.'

I still couldn't say anything. My body felt almost like it was a dead leaf floating on a pond. This was Eunice telling me she loved me. This was the first I'd ever heard about it.

Then she leant even closer, put her lips near my cheek and pressed them on my skin drily. What was she doing?

'I want you to get better. You kids mean the world to me.'

I looked at her blankly. I almost saw a glimmer of a smile on her lips as she looked back at me. I thought I must be hearing things because, in all the time I'd lived with her, she'd never said anything like this, let alone kissed me. Maybe her harsh treatment was for all my own good? Maybe I *was* bad and needed correcting? Perhaps it was tough caring for so many of us, and maybe I was particularly difficult to look after? I suddenly felt that she liked me – she'd even said she loved me – so maybe it was all going to be different from now on.

Relieved, I drifted off to sleep. When I came to again, there was a woman in a blue suit sitting next to the bed. I didn't know her at all but she looked nice and friendly. I felt very thirsty and I tried to sit myself up for a drink. She noticed and got a glass of water for me. After I'd had a drink, the woman sat down again next to me and introduced herself. She was a medical social worker from the hospital and wanted to know how things were living with Eunice. For a moment I couldn't work out what she meant.

'What do you mean?'

The woman paused, smiled and seemed to choose her words carefully. 'Are you happy living with Eunice? Does she treat you well?'

It suddenly flashed before my eyes: the image of Eunice saying 'I love you', stroking my hand and telling me she cared.

'Yes, very well,' I heard myself say.

'No problems, then?'

The woman looked at me, concerned. I could see she wanted to help. But at that moment, in the hospital, I couldn't really think that Eunice was bad any more. Perhaps she had changed? Perhaps what I had done – my desperate suicide attempt – had made her change her mind about me? Maybe we were going to start living like a proper family after all?

I took a long time before I answered.

'No. Not at all.'

Going back home after the hospital I thought things were going to be different, but the minute I got there, I saw that they weren't. Within a day, Eunice was back to her old tricks, dishing out punishments and threatening and then enacting beatings. Things were not going to change. I realized then that she had put on a show in the hospital. I'd had my chance to say something, but in my enfeebled state, I'd been seduced and had missed it.

Eunice never mentioned my suicide attempt – nobody did – but shortly after this Eunice decided that we were going to go on a holiday to America. I'm not sure whether this was a reaction to what had happened with me, or whether she wanted to escape herself from the farm for a while. It wasn't going to be a complete holiday, however. Eunice believed that having a holiday just for its own sake was a sin so we were going to be attending Jehovah's Witness events.

I didn't believe in the Jehovah's Witness religion really. I liked some of the stories, but I hadn't taken it all on for myself. However, going on holiday sounded a good idea, even if we had to do things with Jehovah's Witnesses in tow. It was better than staying on the farm and carrying on as usual.

The money for the trip must have come from John Drake, as there was no other way Eunice would have had the cash she needed for such an ambitious trip. She didn't sell anything and Judith was still living at George Dowty Drive, just the same as ever. Even more bizarre, Eunice decided we would go to Disneyworld and we would spend part of the trip on a cruise ship. When she told us, it seemed unbelievable we would be given such a treat.

I didn't have a passport so Eunice told me to write to my parents – at last – and ask them to fill in a form to get the passport sanctioned. She was breathing down my neck as I obediently wrote saying we would come and visit and bring the papers for them to sign. I had to say we lived on a lovely farm in the countryside (my parents had no idea up until this point that I had spent nearly four whole years at Eckington Bank), and that we had chickens and pigs, a dog and cats and that rural life was fantastic. We must have had a reply (I never saw it, of course), and we all went over to visit my parents.

I can't remember much about the meeting – it's a bit of a blur – but I do remember the first thing my mum said to me was, 'What have you done to your lovely hair?' She was shocked that Eunice had chopped it off as she had expressly told her not to cut it short when I was little. I was wearing a hairband that day, so my hair looked flat on top and I remember my mum being upset by it. I also remember Mum showing me her favourite art books, and some of my drawings from when

I was a little girl, while Dad was on the computer with the other kids. Charlotte wasn't comfortable there and wanted to go, but for once Eunice ignored her as she had business to attend to.

My mum was pretty much occupied by Eunice the whole visit and she finally signed the passport paperwork without question. Eunice had drawn up a contract of sorts concerning me and I think my mum also signed that, giving Eunice many more rights over me than she had had before, like 'parental responsibility'. This was to give her more power and ultimately to make my life more miserable still.

Meanwhile, we were to embark on this extraordinary journey to America for six weeks and we were very excited when we set off for Tampa Bay. Of course, Eunice's main focus was visiting the Jehovah's Witnesses, who were much less reserved than those we knew in the UK, more like gospel preachers. It was weird. We were all very novel to them and they were pleased we'd come such a long way to see them. We really did go to Disneyworld, too, and went on rides, which was amazing.

There were still clouts around the head or bashes on the feet from Eunice during the trip, and we still had poo inspections and squirts of washing-up liquid, but she dropped most of the more elaborate punishment regime, which was a fantastic relief. It was extremely strange to have a real luxury holiday in the middle of all the torture. It almost felt like life had become a bit more normal and I even started to fantasize that maybe Eunice really had changed, maybe a nice Eunice would come back from America and start feeding us properly and treating us well. Perhaps her heart really had been softened when she'd seen me in that hospital bed and she wanted to start afresh?

When we got back to England it was November and it was already cold, with a bite in the air. We came from the warm climate of Florida to a freezing cold farm – we never did have any heating, although Eunice would shut herself in her bedroom with the gas fire blazing – and we went straight back into the old punitive way of life.

Eunice continued to make us children punish each other, but we were a bit older and wiser now and began to get round it by feigning pain. One time Eunice told me to beat Thomas's feet, but I only did it lightly and whispered to him to scream 'Aaaagh!' as if I'd done it very hard. Eunice would be doing something in another room, and I would be meting out the 'punishment', with Thomas on the floor, leg in the air. He and I would use sign language with each other and he would groan on cue, making it sound bad, all the while hoping that Eunice didn't work out what we were doing.

Another time Sarah and I were supposed to go and beat Thomas in the field. We took him out there together, stood around and waited for some time to pass, then went back inside. Eunice asked sternly, 'Did you beat him?' and we nodded meekly that we had. It felt good to get one over on her, a bit like taking back our power, gaining our freedom. I guess as we got older it felt important to win these little victories and feel she was not as all-powerful as she had been when we were really little.

We were still supposed to watch each other all the time but, again, we had begun to give each other a bit more space and freedom. We'd make bargains with each other, like, 'I'll let you do what you want, if you let me do what I want, OK?' Just as long as Eunice didn't get to know, that was always the thing.

We also still took money occasionally – Charlotte was still the only one to get pocket money – and would go on a little raid to the local shops. One day we went to the chemist with some stolen money and bought hairclips, then to the post office for chocolates. Even though it was seldom my idea, I usually got the blame because Eunice always seemed to believe I was the ringleader. Perhaps she sensed that I was more defiant, stronger than Sarah in standing up to her and a bit more rebellious of late. Maybe she was more wary because of the suicide attempt. Who knows?

In actual fact, Charlotte, Eunice's favourite, was usually the one who suggested taking money and she was the very last one that Eunice would ever have suspected. Not that Charlotte got off totally scot-free either. One time she dropped her pocket money when we were all out in a shopping centre and Eunice lifted her skirt and slapped her thigh, which really embarrassed and upset Charlotte. She was seldom in the wrong like that because she was 'pure', having been with Eunice since birth – as was Robert. Knowing I was 'tainted' because – like Thomas and Sarah – I'd been influenced by my parents and that I could never do anything right made me very nervous. I was constantly watching myself, believing I was bad, trying to keep myself on a tight rein.

When I was nearly fourteen I gave Eunice further proof, if proof were needed, of my evil nature. Sarah had once phoned a game line that she'd found in the back of a trade magazine which Eunice had left lying around the house among the clutter. Given there was virtually nothing to read in the house, and I was bored and understimulated most of the time, I, too, found myself flicking through the back of things like *Trade It* magazine where there were loads of game lines you could ring. One day, I decided to give it a go myself, holding my breath as phoning wasn't allowed by Eunice. I must have dialled the wrong number because instead of instructions on how to win money, a woman's voice was talking about the most extraordinary things. I had inadvertently dialled a porn line and was so amazed by what I heard that out of curiosity I kept calling. The women's voices were all soft and sexy, describing things I'd never heard before. It was so weird to hear about sexual intercourse, about oral sex and 'cumming', and I was intrigued. I was an ordinary girl – I fancied boys I saw on the rare occasions we went out and on pop videos I'd seen.

I had so many feelings and questions abut sex that I needed answered, although by then I knew what sexual organs were and I had my periods, obviously.

Sometimes, when I was up all night supposedly doing my homework, I was just dialling the numbers instead, one after the other, over and over. It was a way of keeping myself awake, too. The soft voices sounded so enticing that it was like listening to a short story for seven minutes or so. I kept calling and listening for seven minutes, then I'd call and listen again. But I was too scared to speak.

It didn't make me feel sexy, and I wasn't getting off on the calls. I just had to keep calling because I wanted to understand what was going on. I was utterly fascinated and it took me ages to work out what on earth it was all about. Being so naive, I had no idea what 'I'll make you shoot' and things like that meant. I had worked out by then that willies went into fannies, more or less, but I didn't really know much more than that.

I ran up a £1,000 phone bill. Eunice went utterly ballistic and dialled the itemized numbers. She confronted me and I said, 'It was just a game'. She then said, 'There are a lot of things you need to know'. I thought, *Well, you should be telling me, then.* I felt more feisty than usual because I was beginning to grow up.

After a vicious beating, during which she had held me down with her foot on my neck so she could get the stick into my mouth, Eunice marched me round to the local shop – the very one where we had gone on our spending sprees – and told them, in front of me, why I needed a job to pay off a debt. Eunice explained – in detail – what I had done and I was very embarrassed indeed. It seemed worse because it was something a boy would usually do, but in my ignorance, or rather, total naivety, I had ended up getting myself into huge debt, without realizing at all what I was doing. Eunice was not going to let this one pass and the issue of the debt would rumble on for a very long time. Like the proverbial elephant, Eunice never forgot. Especially when it came to something 'evil' perpetrated by me.

CHAPTER 16: *Tragedy*

I was always a small-framed, slim child; even now as a fully grown adult, my feet are still only size three, I'm under 1.5 metres tall and only just a size eight. As a teenager, I was probably about the size of a healthy ten-year-old. I'm sure some of this is down to genes, but it must be due in part to malnourishment, as with the other children.

Under Eunice's regime I became a binge eater, largely because that's how she trained us up. There would be food for a few days, then no food, so I had to learn to live without it. I had to learn not to feel hunger, in the same way that I had to suppress pain when the beatings went on and on and on. If I had felt the hunger or the pain I would have gone insane.

Even after I escaped Eunice's control I would lapse into unhealthy eating patterns. For instance, if I binged on chocolate I would not eat at all for two whole days to compensate. These sorts of behaviours were set up by Eunice in my childhood through her completely inappropriate treatment. She didn't try to teach me, or any of the other children, how to eat well or look after ourselves and our health. She did the complete opposite of what you should do with children in terms of teaching them about sensible eating. It has taken me a very long time to get to grips with healthy eating. As an adult and a mum, I've had to learn how to eat a balanced diet both for myself and for my growing daughter's sake.

By the time I was fourteen, Eunice noticed I enjoyed being skinny and not having to eat because it made me feel more attractive, even with short hair. She got it into her head that I was now probably anorexic. I'm sure she was right – that I was beginning to see food as a means of taking back control. But I was only doing this because I had been so terribly and confusingly controlled by Eunice. As ever, she saw my problem as my fault, and nothing to do with her.

Since happiness was not allowed by Eunice, now that I wanted to be thin, she decided maliciously that she had to do something about it. It wouldn't be something to help me, or be pleasant for me, obviously. Quite the opposite. Eunice had a new eating plan: I was to eat lard. A whole pound before every meal. One day I came into the kitchen and Eunice was standing by the table, hands on her hips with a determined look on her face. I was in for it.

'Sit down.'

I sat down, as commanded. Rather like Jet would 'sit' when Eunice snapped her orders at him. Eunice went over to the counter, then returned to the table and there, glistening on a plate, was a whole slab of solid white lard. I looked at it in horror. Eunice watched my face closely, as I swallowed hard.

'You're to eat it. All of it. Every mealtime, I want you to eat a pound of lard. You need fattening up.'

I knew better than to respond, but as I looked at the block of fat my stomach heaved. It looked disgusting – I couldn't possibly put that stuff in my mouth. I'd really rather die.

'Go on. Eat.'

Eunice was not budging. Her face was set in its usual grimace of rigid determination. Her eyes gleamed cruelly behind her glasses. I'd been here a million times and it was yet another battle of wills. The other children gathered at the kitchen door and watched in horror as I took the spoon. I sliced into the solid fat and brought a slimy spoonful to my lips. They wouldn't open, but oily, piggy odour wafted up to my nose. *I can't eat this, I just can't. I'm going to throw up. Please don't make me. Please.* I said nothing and stared at the spoon, wanting it to disappear in a puff of smoke.

'Eat it. Now. Or do I have to make you?'

I opened my mouth and put in the spoon. Almost instantly the fatty mass started melting and sliding over my tongue and teeth, coating them with grease, then it slipped down the back of my throat, tasting of oily sausages. It was vile and made me want to retch. Eunice stood over me, almost willing me to be sick, or to protest. *I can't swallow. I can't.*

'Swallow.'

I forced it down and instantly felt my stomach churning as the greasy mass hit my system. I dug into the lard again and, blanking out my mind, raised the next revolting spoonful to my lips, trying not to experience it as it melted on my tongue. *I want to be sick. I'm gonna retch.*

'Swallow.'

I could feel the other children's eyes riveted on me in morbid fascination as I managed to work my way through about a quarter of the block, trying to stop myself being sick at every mouthful. They knew it could be them next, so they said not a word. When I chewed, I retched automatically, as the grease spread around my mouth, so I had to quickly swallow back down the rising contents of my stomach. I had really never eaten anything so revolting in all my life. Even the rat-poo porridge was not as bad as having to fill my mouth and my system with this stinking, oily gunge.

Satisfied with my obedience, Eunice finally turned away, busying herself at the counter, clearly believing that I was now conquered. I quickly spat out everything from my mouth into a paper towel and tucked it under my bottom on my seat. Eunice turned back and I sat up, looking innocent. Then she went out of the room, followed by the other children. Thinking quickly, I grabbed the block and threw it across the room, over the cooker, where it disappeared into an open space in the alcove behind, where a range used to be.

Other times, when Eunice left me with a plate of lard to consume before a meal, I would come prepared with toilet paper pushed into my pants. When she wasn't looking I'd retrieve the paper, wrap the lard up quickly, dirtying the spoon first, of course, then I'd pretend I'd eaten it all. As soon as I could I would rush out, over the lawn, past the barn and across the open field, where I would lob the lard as far as I could over the hedge. Sometimes I was seen by Charlotte and I would pray silently that she wouldn't tell because I knew my lard nightmare would only increase if she did. She did tell on me once, having seen me throw the lard over the field from her bedroom window. I had an extra beating and an extra dose of lard as a consequence.

Luckily, neither Eunice nor her spies could watch me all the time and I had become clever at dealing with the lard. Sometimes I would microwave it to melt it down so I could drink it; it was still awful, but I had to try something to get it down. Then I could even pour a little bit down the sink if no one was there. I would risk anything because, to be honest, I would rather have starved than eat the stuff. It was so sickening that even to this day, the very thought of it, the very smell of anything like it, makes me instantly want to throw up. It's also made it hard for me to cook with oil or taste anything that is slightly fatty. Even the smell of sausages cooking or fast food outlets turns my stomach.

*

The renovation of the farm – which seemed to take for ever – had reached the kitchen. All the quarry tiles had been removed and new concrete foundations were being laid. In fact, most of the household furniture had been moved out to the barn and Eunice had almost gutted the place. She was also planning to convert the attic into a loft space. New staircases were built and we were living, largely, on a building site.

Judith was involved in the project because she worked as a secretary at a builders merchants and her boss had been roped in to help out with the planning and refurbishment. Judith was often at the farm now and the living conditions had become even worse, if that was at all possible. It had always been cold, but it was now tougher and rougher. There was still a caravan on site and Judith sometimes slept in it. As always, I still slept on the floor, just on a doubled-over quilt with a dirty, old sofa cushion, still with no proper bedding or privacy, even though I was nearing fifteen.

We had a pet goose, a duck and a rabbit, all of which lived in the house with us. I had two cats then – an epileptic one called Posey and an old one called Poppy. Judith had one called Gobbelino, which lived at the farm with us, too. Before the kitchen floor was lifted up, I had been sleeping under the kitchen table with the goose and duck in a box of hay beside me and the rabbit in a little cage. (I was always moving from the living room to the kitchen and back again, according to which of my tasks was uppermost in Eunice's mind at the time.) I felt at home with the animals which I looked after lovingly (a good sight better than Eunice ever cared for me), so I liked sleeping with them in the kitchen. It was better than having to tend to Robert all night in the living room, anyway.

There was a period around this time when I was left at the farm with Judith for a while, so I could look after the animals, while Eunice took the others back to George Dowty Drive. Judith was good with her hands and she was making wooden furniture for the farm – she was quite skilful. Life was a hell of a lot better with Judith than it was when Eunice was around. It was almost pleasant. Although Judith did hold us down for beatings or carry out other punishments, it was usually only when Eunice told her to do it. On her own Judith wasn't that bad, especially away from Eunice's evil influence. I never dared ask her why she thought her mother was so horrible to children or why she stayed at home so long. Neither did I manage to find out why Judith's younger sister left and wasn't in touch any more. I wasn't used to asking questions, so I kept quiet, as I'd been trained to.

However, life for all of us, was about to come crashing down. It was in September 2000 that Eunice decided we were going to have a short break of four days away at Pontin's Holiday Camp at Brean Sands, near Weston-super-Mare, on the coast. Judith joined us in her Bedford Rascal and brought a couple of Jehovah's Witness friends to the resort. It was not a holiday on the grand scale of our trip to Disneyworld – that was truly a one-off – and we just lived in an apartment for the weekend. Although there was a funfair and things to do, we weren't really allowed out to explore and have fun. I was in Eunice's Bad Books that weekend as I had forgotten to bring the washing-up liquid, so I was being punished. I got a clout in the mouth, plus Eunice had developed a new delightful habit of kicking me in the shins when she was annoyed, perhaps as I was getting a bit too big for her to beat my feet very easily. She kicked me whenever she felt like it and I was often left with big bruises on my legs as a consequence.

One night we went out to the social club, where there was a disco (Eunice hardly went wild, drinking only half a shandy) and we also watched a puppet show, but we were largely prisoners in the apartment, and it very much like being at home rather than being on holiday. There were no special treats either.

On the last night, as we were packing up to go home, Robert lost his temper and threw a toy digger at me. It hit my eyebrow, splitting it open. Blood was pouring everywhere, and Eunice got very annoyed at the mess. Judith's Jehovah's Witness friend who was with us at the time said I ought to go to First Aid as the cut was deep, plus to check if I had concussion. She also told Eunice I would probably need stitches as the cut was pretty big.

'I'm not doing that, she's perfectly fine,' said Eunice, as ever the concerned carer.

Judith's friend remonstrated with her, as my clothes were spattered with blood and I was clearly dazed, saying that at least I shouldn't travel. Eunice roughly pulled the edges of my cut eyebrow together and stuck them together with butterfly plasters, irritated by my having caused so much trouble. No anaesthetic or words of comfort, of course. She tugged hard at the tender skin as she held my wound in place. I was made to feel that *I* had done something terrible. Amazingly, Robert didn't get told off at all: it was all my fault, yet again.

The upshot was that we stayed an extra night at Pontin's and Eunice was pretty annoyed about the whole thing – I guess because of the extra cost and also because she didn't like anyone interfering in her plans. I knew better than to show that my injury hurt or to ask for any comfort or care; I just had to put up with it and stay quiet.

The next day after breakfast, having finally packed up our apartment to go home, it was agreed that Judith, Robert, Charlotte and Sarah would go swimming on the way back, while Eunice, Thomas and I would go via the cattery to pick up the animals. I asked if I could go swimming, too, but Eunice looked outraged and snapped that I was still in her Bad Books, so I had work to do.

Thinking about it now, I probably couldn't have gone swimming because of my cut, but I just wanted to extend the holiday, have some fun and get away from Eunice, because returning to the farm always filled me with dread. However,

Eunice told me I had to go straight home and look after the animals. I knew better than to argue with Eunice, or show her that I cared in any way, so we drove home in silence. But I did love my animals and looked forward to seeing them again.

It got to about teatime that day and we had stopped at Eunice's mum's bungalow for a lovely supper of spaghetti Bolognese. However, after supper we had still not heard from the others, which was odd, but we thought they must have got held up. There was a big shopping precinct near to Pershore and Eunice said, sarcastically, that she bet Judith had stopped off there to do some clothes shopping and that she'd kill her if she had.

A couple of hours later we still had not heard anything, and by now it was very strange. Maybe Judith had gone a different route and had got stuck in traffic, but she would have called as she had a mobile. Eunice tried phoning Judith but there was no answer.

We were not allowed TV or radio at Eunice's mum's either, so we didn't know what was on the news. However, at around eight or nine o'clock the phone rang. It was one of the Jehovah's Witnesses who Eunice knew from the Kingdom Hall in Tewkesbury, calling to check that Judith was OK. They had watched the news on TV that teatime and had seen a report about a multiple car smash; they thought they had recognized Judith's car among the vehicles.

Eunice called Frenchay Hospital and found out that

everyone was there. I could hear her asking if they were alive or dead and when she came back she was pale and grim-faced, but didn't say anything to me. Instead she just went round the room thumping things while I watched her. I knew better than to ask anything.

Then Eunice disappeared in her mustard Volvo Estate and I stayed the night with Katie. Thomas stayed with me, too. None of the grown-ups told us anything at all, so we felt very confused. The next day, two Jehovah's Witnesses came to fetch us and we were driven to Frenchay Hospital, in silence. It was all very mysterious, but I did sense that something had gone dreadfully wrong. I just didn't know what, which was even worse.

When Thomas and I arrived we were taken into a little room and Eunice came in, looking very frosty. I don't know why I remember that I was wearing a pink and white checked top and a pair of old jeans. I had no idea what Eunice was going to say, but it was clear from her white, drawn face that it would be bad. She simply stood in front of us, without emotion and gave it to us without any preparation: 'Judith and Charlotte are dead. Sarah is critical and probably won't make it through the night and Robert is in the High Dependency Unit.'

I burst into tears. Dead? Judith, dead? And Charlotte? Just like that? I couldn't believe it. I was in utter shock. Judith! Charlotte! I'd lived with them for years, and although I hadn't always got on with either of them, especially Charlotte, they were, well, like family. The only family I apparently had now, anyway. The tears flowed as Eunice told us bluntly what had happened. She continued to stand apart from us – no hugs, no kisses, no comfort – and told us that Judith's car had been totally crushed.

'They were waiting in a traffic jam on the M5 and the lorry driver behind was fiddling with his radio or something – he just didn't see them. Anyway, he didn't stop, just ploughed on into them.'

As she spoke I imagined the scene in graphic detail. I couldn't stop shaking as I pictured the smash, the blood, the screams, the sound of glass and bones breaking. Were they awake? Did they feel it all? Did they experience their lives ebbing away, and what was it like waiting for the ambulance? I pictured Judith driving, Charlotte sitting next to her, maybe chatting as Judith was always more fun than Eunice to travel home with, and Sarah and Robert in the back, looking out of the window, relaxed after swimming. They would have been looking forward to teatime at Eunice's mum's, which was always better than being at the farm. I kept thinking, if only they hadn't gone swimming, they'd still be alive. I could not really understand that I would never, ever see them again. It was so absolute, so sudden and so final.

Eunice said when the lorry hit them full-on from behind – it was a 24-tonne vehicle – it shunted the back of the Rascal over the front two seats, which were crushed flat, killing Judith and Charlotte outright. The two back seats were left sort of dangling over the front ones, with Robert and Sarah hanging precariously by their seatbelts, very seriously injured and bleeding. Robert had broken both his legs and ended up with four pins in each, while Sarah had multiple fractures of the spine and pelvis and internal injuries. She needed a blood transfusion but being brought up as a Jehovah's Witness meant she was refused one by Eunice, which nearly killed her. It was touch and go if she would live.

When Eunice got to the end of the terrible story, she turned and focused her piercing gaze on me:

'It's all your fault, Harriet,' she said. 'If you hadn't cut your eye we would have left a day earlier. You're to blame. They were my two angels, and they died. You two are the Devil's kids, which is why you've been saved.'

I was devastated by her words. If I could have died on the spot, I would have at that dreadful moment. The weight of the blame was like being crushed under an enormous stone. I could hardly breathe, let alone think. I should have been in that car. I should have been crushed to death instead of Judith, Eunice's own daughter, or Charlotte, her favourite. Of course, the accident and the deaths were my fault. Everything always was.

CHAPTER 17: *Aftermath*

Life was never going to be the same after the crash. I was obviously very shocked and upset by the deaths of Charlotte and Judith and I cried masses at their funerals. It was very hard to adjust to their having been wiped out so suddenly and completely; I just wasn't prepared for anything like it. Plus, Sarah and Robert were terribly hurt. In fact Sarah nearly died. I had to get used to life without them being around at home for a long while, as well.

Eunice's parents took Thomas and myself in while Eunice stayed in hospital with Robert and Sarah during their recovery, which took several long months. Eunice's parents were far nicer to live with than Eunice and would give us treats, like sweets. Unfortunately Eunice knew we were getting sweets from them and said we weren't allowed to eat them; so whenever we saw her we'd have to empty our pockets and hand them all over. We felt we couldn't refuse the sweets from Katie, though, as we were told it would be rude, so it was torture to have them, but not be able to eat them.

In a way Eunice's parents were like substitute grandparents at the time. They were quite strict Jehovah's Witnesses, especially her dad, who now had arthritis and sat in a wheelchair most of the time, but I don't think they had any idea how violent and bizarre their daughter's behaviour was towards us. Eunice was still clouting us, even though we were living with her parents. I remember her mum asking me if Eunice hit us, and I just said 'No'. I knew better than to own up, as more beatings or even worse would follow if Eunice found out.

Once Sarah and Robert had recovered enough to leave hospital, we went back to living mainly at George Dowty Drive. Eunice wouldn't let us use Charlotte or Judith's rooms, so Thomas and I still had to share. She kept their rooms as a shrine, allowing nothing to be moved, but making me dust them occasionally. George Dowty was still a dirty mess and the attic was still full of not only her daughters' clothes, but also Eunice's old things from the sixties and seventies. Every toy from their childhood was there, too, and the house was like a museum of all those – children and men alike – who had passed through. So now that two of them were dead, I could imagine Eunice would keep their rooms as they were for ever.

Amazingly, Charlotte's birth parents were not told about the crash or her death by the hospital as Eunice was her adoptive mother. When they found out by reading the local paper, they wrote a letter to Eunice, furious that they had not been informed about the accident sooner and saying that she'd had no right to keep it from them. Eunice was unmoved. It was yet another example of her desire to control everybody and everything.

It was similar with me: there were times when we drove past the end of my parents' road and I would wonder, wistfully, if I would ever see them again. It seemed so strange to know they were there, but to have no contact with them whatsoever. What were they doing? Was my nan still alive? Did they ever think about? Did they miss me? Had they any idea what kind of life I was leading? Eunice would say to me nastily, 'You will go back to them, the minute you can,' to try to goad me into staying loyal to her and her way of thinking. And she was still always rude about them, saying they were useless, terrible people and, by implication, I was just the same – it was obviously in the blood.

We were still having our poos checked every morning but Eunice now often left it to me to check Thomas, who often couldn't produce to order. I would just tell her, 'Yeah, he's done it,' to keep her happy whether he had or not. I suppose I was beginning to feel I was big enough to handle the situation, even if there was a risk.

Occasionally, we'd go over to the farm to oversee the building and decorating work. A local villager was looking after my chickens and the black pigs, Bunty and Bessie. Some of the cats had died, but we took the duck, goose and rabbit back to George Dowty with us, where they lived in a straw-filled box under the table in the kitchen. I usually had to sleep with them there, too.

Sarah had only just survived the accident, but she was severely injured and came home in a wheelchair, unable to walk at first. She had to have a colostomy bag for some time, which was really difficult for a teenage girl to cope with. However, Eunice was not particularly kind to her when she came home. She forced her to remain wheelchair-bound for some *four years* after she could actually walk. I now realize this was probably so that she could claim some kind of disability carer's allowance. It might also have been that there was going to be a compensation claim and Eunice might have thought that if Sarah couldn't walk the pay-out would be higher. (I read in the press that Sarah ended up with a settlement of £5,000, which Eunice kept and used to buy a new fireplace.) It's also possible that Eunice thought, in her typical punitive way, that Sarah should have died instead of the other two, so she would extend Sarah's misery for as long as she could.

Robert had also sustained terrible injuries and it took him a long time before he could walk properly again. But one extraordinary thing was revealed to the world outside the farm as a result of the accident: that Eunice had kept Robert in nappies even though he was now about eight. (He was still having a bottle of 7UP at night before bed, too). I had just accepted this as part of Eunice's warped desire to keep Robert a 'pure' baby for ever, but once the nurses in the hospital saw it, I realized how odd it must have looked. It was very embarrassing for Robert to have this exposed in hospital. Of course he stopped wearing nappies while he was there as the hospital staff must have seen it as totally abnormal for a child of his age. What's amazing, though, is that this didn't alert someone to look into Eunice's treatment of the rest of us in any more detail. It was a crucial time when the authorities failed to pick up vital clues. But it wasn't the first.

While we were living again at George Dowty, I threw a diary I had written over the fence onto the man next door's back lawn. I had written it deliberately, showing how we were living, and I had written in it, 'Please help me, please help us'. Imagine my intense disappointment when a few days later the diary was simply tossed back over to our side of the fence. Absolutely nothing happened. I wonder now, if I were to find something similar in my back garden whether I would do the same? Or would I take it seriously and either go and knock on the door and see what was happening, or take the diary down to the local police station, if I thought going there myself too risky? But could I just ignore it? Or, worse, just throw it back over the fence onto the lawn for the persecutor to find? That seems the most bizarre reaction of all.

I suppose it's possible that the neighbour might not have read it; he might have just thrown it back without looking at it. But it made me feel that absolutely nobody cared about our plight – not even those who lived right next to us – and that there was no hope. Surely they must have heard our screams? They must have seen that we were always around, and not at school, and that we were dressed shabbily, looked scrawny, pale and thin and were often covered with bruises? It is amazing to me that in a neighbourhood with houses in such close proximity, the aggression that went on day and night could have gone on completely unnoticed. Or maybe people did notice but were scared of getting involved, worried about the consequences or of wrongly accusing Eunice? Maybe she frightened the adults around us as much she did us? Whatever the reason, nothing was done, and Eunice was able to carry out her daily violations without anyone's interference.

Eunice had stopped starving us so much, and was still trying to fatten me up on lard, but it was difficult for her to do that regularly by then as a lot of our usual routines had been disrupted by the accident. Also, there were other people around, like her mum and dad, and hospital staff when we visited the others, so she had to be a bit more careful about what she got up to. However, I still looked gaunt, skinny and hollow-eyed because I was developing anorexia and was also still taking Ritalin at night.

One morning, Eunice came barging unexpectedly into mine and Thomas's room when I was still only half awake.

Her hands were hidden behind her back and she looked incredibly tense and fierce. I knew something was up, which brought me to my senses very quickly.

Eunice held up an empty pill bottle. 'What's this?'

I'd finished off Robert's supply the previous night and I must have got careless and left the bottle lying around as evidence. I said nothing and tried to stay very still.

'You evil little drug addict,' spat out Eunice venomously. She came over to where I'd been sleeping on the floor and pulled the duvet off me, then bent down and grabbed me by the arm. I struggled, but could feel her bony fingers boring into my upper arm.

'You're not to be trusted, you demonized scum. Where are the pills?'

I still said nothing – what could I say? I could see Eunice was beside herself with fury. She was pulling me across the room, and trying to grab handfuls of hair.

'You ungrateful drug addict. You're evil, that's what you are, evil scum. You're utterly untrustworthy. How dare you think you can do this to me? You need teaching a lesson you'll never forget.'

I was pulled out of the room by my hair and kicked down the stairs to the living room, where Eunice locked me in, got the bamboo stick and beat me and beat me until she was exhausted herself. She kicked me around the room, pummelling me with her fists until I just went limp, taking her blows.

I knew better than to fight, although in my mind I wanted to stand up and beat her back. I wanted to hit her and hit her and never stop hitting her, to shut up her nasty mouth and blacken her hateful eyes. But I didn't. I controlled myself, as ever, and took the punishment.

Inside, however, I felt even more resentful, especially when she gave the pills to Sarah to look after once she came home from hospital for good. It was a great wrench for me to have to suddenly give them up. I felt dreadful, not only from the beating, but from the withdrawal symptoms that gave me the shakes and made me feel grumpy and unsettled. I couldn't get to sleep at night and I was desperate because my only source of comfort and escape had now been taken away.

Another incident stands out, only in this case it's because it was one of the rare times that I did fight back. I was being punished – for a change – and Eunice was sitting across my chest. I was on the floor, with her thighs either side of me. She was pinning me down, her hands holding down my puny arms. I remember the strong stench of her armpits, which stank, as always (of course, she didn't believe in using deodorants). She freed one hand to push my lower lip onto my lower teeth – as ever, it really hurt and I could taste the blood in my mouth. For some reason, on this day, I'd had enough, and with my free hand I clawed her bottom.

I could see from her eyes that she was shocked as she

shouted, 'How dare you?' and started to clout me around the head and face. Soon I was a mass of bruises and cuts. But I really must have been angry that day because I didn't care and just continued to claw and claw at her big, fat, wobbly bottom. She was going to hurt me anyway, so I thought I might as well do some damage. That must have been my logic.

We were never allowed to answer back, and certainly not allowed to fight back, so Eunice must have been outraged, which was why she lost it so completely. In the middle of it all she told me to hold still so she could clout me properly, so I wouldn't bruise. But I was having none of it and continued to wriggle and claw. I didn't care. At some point I bit her knuckle – or it got grazed on my teeth – and shortly after the cut got infected. I remember Eunice showing me the infection afterwards and saying she'd got it because I was diseased and that some people like me were born with evil in them, which you just couldn't get rid of.

That beating must have been very tough because it put me off fighting back for nearly another two years. She had pummelled my head over and over and just kept hitting me until I was pulped. She'd actually lost her temper, which was unusual, as she was normally very cold and calculated. I felt I'd been knocked into place and that my spirit had been broken. But I think Eunice was shocked that I'd dared to claw her bum – I think we both were – and that she might have realized then, that as I got bigger, I would eventually be able to fight back properly.

Eunice obviously needed to shift her game a bit. Now I was a proper teenager, sex would come up occasionally and she would have to make her feelings known. The phone-lines bill at the farm was a big black mark against me and she still continually pressed me to pay her back. Then, one day, I was standing in the utility room by the washing machine, when Eunice came in. At my feet, among all the clutter, was a newspaper with a picture of a topless woman in it. Eunice's eagle eye alighted on it and she picked it up. I thought, *Uh-oh, I'm in for it now,* even though I knew I hadn't gone out and bought the newspaper. It might well have been a freebie. Later, I would understand that newspapers and magazines used images of naked women to sell all sorts of things, but at that time I'd been so isolated from the world I had no idea that this kind of image was on show absolutely everywhere, every day.

Well, Eunice lost it big time. She started kicking me over and over in my crotch. It hurt like hell – I was only wearing a thin shell suit (which I'd got secondhand from a charity shop, of course) – and I was pinned against the washing machine so I couldn't move away. Eunice just kicked and kicked and kicked. I thought I would pass out from the pain. This was Eunice's own original brand of sex education, for sure, although I'm not sure exactly what it was supposed to be teaching me.

However, Eunice did persist in trying to get me together with her friend Kevin. She would say things like, 'Why don't you go for a walk together with Kevin?' I found out that originally he'd been a heavy drinker and that he'd recently started to drink again. Eunice hoped to straighten him out and somehow she saw me as the means to keep him under control.

Now that I was sixteen I think he saw me as fair game. He became progressively ruder and more suggestive with me. It was a real nightmare. If we went for a walk with the dog, he would try to hold my hand, or would grab at me in some way or say things like, 'You look very sexy in those shorts today.' He'd be drooling over me and I'd think, *Yeah, to boys my age, but not to you, mate.*

Once, he said (about another woman near by) 'I bet she's got a nice pussy.' I felt disgusted. Why was he talking this way to me? What did he expect me to do or say? 'I don't wanna know,' I said. 'You go and find out.'

'No, she ain't got big enough boobs,' he said. Kevin really made my skin creep.

He grabbed my breasts once, and I was revolted by Kevin's assault. It was a horrible moment as I struggled to get away from him. I was dishevelled and feeling sick. I went in search of Eunice who was sitting inside, peeling an apple. I wouldn't usually say anything to her, or make a fuss about anything, but I was furious about being left with this pest. I went and stood in front of Eunice.

'I don't want to be on my own with him any more.'

Eunice didn't stop peeling or look up at me. There was a moment's pause.

'Why not?' She took a bite of her apple and looked out of the door to where Kevin was still standing. 'I just don't like him.'

'Well, he really likes you; you make him feel better.'

I felt resentful and for once I spoke out. 'I don't want to be on my own with him, or sit next to him, or be put with him or be anywhere with him.'

Eunice glanced up at me, straight-faced, then bit into her apple again. She didn't offer to do anything or to protect me from Kevin in any way. Later, when I was driven to distraction by his constant pawing, I told her blatantly what he was doing to me and she went berserk at him.

Once I made it very clear to him – and to Eunice – that his advances were absolutely not wanted (I thought I had made it clear all along, but he had continued to persist regardless) he finally got the message

Looking back, I realize that Eunice must have come into the rest of John Drake's property when Charlotte died. As he had left the farm to Charlotte in a trust, her death must have meant the farm was passed on to her 'next of kin' – Eunice. I didn't understand it properly at the time, but Eunice had big money to spend finally.

I was sixteen when, one afternoon, we were driving in the Volvo and ended up down by the marina in Tewkesbury. We all sat in the car and waited while Eunice went down to see the boats. When she came back to the car she announced, 'I've eyed up a boat; I might buy one.' We were all astounded. Buy one? I kept my face blank, but inside I was thinking, *Buy a boat? How can you buy a boat? Where'd you get that amount of money from?* But I knew better than to ask.

A few days later Eunice picked up her father, who was in a wheelchair, and we all went to have a look at the boat together. We got to a mooring place and there was a barge with the name 'Charlotte' on the side. I realized immediately the significance for Eunice. The barge was 70-foot long, apparently the longest you could get. It had a wheelchair lift, which Eunice tried out with her father and Sarah. She seemed pleased that she could get the wheelchair users on and off the boat quite easily, although the barge itself was really quite massive. She kept saying, 'I'm going to buy this boat' over and over like a mantra. The barge was priced at £40,000 but I heard that in the end she'd haggled them down to £37,000. She seemed very pleased with herself, but I was still amazed that she could afford it. All these years we'd lived in penury, never having much food, no heating, few holidays, no new clothes, no trips out or any new toys.

She had bullied me for months over my phone bill, but she really was rolling in it now. It seemed she was suddenly rich, if she could afford to buy a boat, for £37,000. Just like that.

Having bought the barge, Eunice decided we would go on a six-week holiday. First we had to clean it up – I was used to cleaning by then, so I had to roll up my sleeves and start scrubbing. Then Eunice had to organize someone to look after the farm animals while we were away, because we were now living half at the farm and half at George Dowty, going back and forth between the two. I felt sad saying goodbye to my chickens and pigs, cats and other farmyard pets, apart from Jet, who came with us, but I suppose I was a bit excited that we were doing something new. It's hard to explain, but in a life like mine, where so much that was horrible happened all the time, on a daily basis, just a small change, a little bit of something nice or different, went a very long way indeed.

We set off on our barge holiday with Eunice, her mum and dad, us four children. We also took with us six rabbits and a goldfish called Marigold in a bowl (Eunice's pet), so we must have looked like a band of gypsies. I was allowed to have a go at steering the barge at some point early on in our trip, and I bumped the goldfish out of the bowl when I knocked into the lock. It was quite comic and I took some pleasure in the upset it gave Eunice, although I was sad about the fish. It was a lovely goldfish.

At this point Eunice was getting on better with me; she might have worried that I'd blow the whistle at some point or, at least, begin to fight back. Even though she had conditioned me to be terrified of her over the years, I'd got used to her by now, and I was managing to risk a bit of argy-bargy every so often. I was beginning gather the strength to be more assertive, to talk back and stand my ground. It was getting to the point where I would threaten her as she hit me, saying, 'I'm an adult now, you can't carry on doing this to me. I'm gonna tell on you.' I was also much more snappy and moody in general and less co-operative when she wanted me to do something, and very fed up about not being allowed pocket money, music, radio, TV, magazines, make-up, new clothes or anything teenagers usually had. She wouldn't let me have a life and I was becoming very resentful about it. It was only in small ways, but I had been so dominated by her for so long that even the smallest shifts really were mountainous.

We were heading up the Llangollen Canal in Wales very slowly and one day during the trip we were going over an incredibly narrow aqueduct, called Pontcysyllte. It was 305 metres long and 39 metres above the valley below with magnificent views over the surrounding countryside. I'd never seen anything like it, and you could walk along it on a narrow path beside the barge. I wanted to see the view, so I got off and walked. The scenery was really fantastic, although I'm petrified of heights and felt I might be swept off any minute by a gust of wind, or I might just fall if I looked too far over the side of the aqueduct.

The holiday ended up lasting from September 2001 until March 2002, and did give me a taste of real freedom. I was allowed to walk the dog alone, just the two of us on the tow-path. I could breathe the air, look at the sky, think my own thoughts and simply experience being solitary, without having someone's gaze on me all the time. I only began to realize through these walks what it had been like to be watched constantly by Eunice, to have to be careful, accountable, all the time.

So my stolen moments of freedom, when I could stroll and look at a bird take flight, or watch the evening sky, helped a new feeling to form in my soul, and made a new idea crystallize in my mind. It felt scary to contemplate it, but also exciting to imagine. And I always had a very active imagination.

I was almost seventeen and beginning to feel the time had come for me to leave what passed for a home.

CHAPTER 18: *Abandoned*

The months spent away had broken the bond with my old life, just as the deaths of Charlotte and Judith had somehow broken Eunice's desire to keep us all cooped up, enslaved at her beck and call on the farm. I had no idea what lay 'out there' in the world beyond, because the Jehovah's Witnesses, through Eunice, had always made sure that the outside environment would remain both hostile and dangerous. In addition to anything the Jehovah's Witnesses believed, I'd been told by Eunice for years that I wouldn't live past the age of ten (although I obviously did), that I was evil, unworthy and diseased, so I thought I wouldn't live very long in the outside world anyway.

I had learned to skivvy, cook, clean, tend animals and be kicked around, but being able to talk to or trust people, make friends, work out finances or look after myself properly – this was completely foreign territory. Thus, the idea of launching myself into the unknown was totally daunting. Nevertheless, I had reached an emotional and psychological crossroads now and there was no real turning back. At sixteen going on seventeen, I'd got the whiff of freedom in my nostrils and wanted to explore it further.

I was impatient to get away and started to drop enormous hints to Eunice. I was even daring to badger her. I'd never asked for anything before, or expressed any desires, but the urge to leave got stronger and stronger as every day went by. I think Eunice could smell rebellion on me and she probably knew she'd have to do something about it soon.

After the barge trip we went back to living at the farm. The whole place was like a building site, a total tip. There would be a burst of activity for a few days, such as some plastering, then it would stop and we'd be left with the mess. Eunice was living now in the caravan. Sarah was still confined to her wheelchair (although she could have walked) and Robert was hobbling but mobile, and they had been given rooms. Thomas and I were put on the dirty, cold floor, wherever we could find a space, and were back to sleeping in a folded-over quilt and an ancient sofa cushion.

These days, when Eunice tried to beat me, I always tried to get her back in some subtle way, by catching her with my nail or my teeth, or even trying to trip her up or hurt her back. I was gradually coming to the boil. I didn't want to hurt her badly, but I was sick of her random violence, and wanted to be free of her constant psychological domination.

One day, Sarah and I put a Ritalin pill in Eunice's tea to

see what would happen. We stirred it round till it melted. We were terrified about what would happen if she tasted it and twigged what we were doing, but luckily, she didn't. She just got sleepy and said, uncharacteristically, 'Oh, I feel a bit tired today.' It was a real relief seeing her nod off in her chair, something she almost never did. It gave us a little peace for a while, enabling us to go off and listen to the radio or even sneak a look at a teen magazine like ordinary teenagers (we'd smuggled it into the house), without her beady eye on us.

Meanwhile, I kept saying I wanted to leave and Eunice kept ignoring me. I nagged and nagged as I felt I would explode otherwise; I think she must have got fed up with it because one day, when we were in the kitchen together and I was feeding Jet while she was making some tea, she said, 'You'll be leaving tomorrow, so you better get yourself sorted.'

I nearly fell over with shock. What did she mean? Where was I going?

'Where to?'

'You want to leave, you can leave,' was all she said, mysteriously. 'Be ready by nine in the morning – I'll drive you.' Then she walked out of the kitchen and I knew better than to ask any more.

I rushed upstairs and found some clothes and other stuff. I had virtually no possessions – no smart bag or new clothes, no special pieces of jewellery (my gold heart with the rose was lost by then), souvenirs or piggy-bank savings. I didn't have a suitcase, so I stuffed my few belongings into a black plastic bag.

I was going. I was being freed.

Eunice told me not to say anything, that the other children weren't to know I was going, which meant I couldn't say goodbye. I had no mobile phone, no money. I hadn't really thought through the practicalities at all. Would Eunice give me help? I had no idea. I knew I'd have to get a job, but I'd do anything to survive.

The next day, Eunice told Thomas and Robert that we were taking Sarah for her hospital appointment. She took Sarah out to the minivan she'd bought while I stood awkwardly with the two boys, wanting to say something but not knowing how to express any warm emotions. 'I'll see you soon,' was all I could muster as I climbed into the van and went through the farm's five-bar gate for the last time. I looked back and waved at Thomas and Robert, then the farm disappeared as the car drove round the bend and I set off for my new life, wherever it was to be.

We drove in silence for about fifteen minutes, while I took in the enormity of my leaving. Eunice was intent on driving, but I was feeling a mixture of complete terror and excitement in equal measure.

'I'm taking you to Bristol,' Eunice piped up suddenly.

'Bristol? I don't know Bristol? Why not Cheltenham or Tewkesbury?'

I seldom questioned her decisions, so this felt new. She was evasive though.

'You'll be in a youth hostel. I'll pay your rent for a month.'

Eunice carried on driving. I said nothing while I took this in. Why Bristol? Clearly Eunice didn't want me to be in Cheltenham, because of the possibility of meeting my parents, or in Tewkesbury, because other people would twig she'd let me leave home. Above all, she must have been terrified that I would spill the beans about her cruel regime.

'You'll be back after that, tail between your legs.'

Ah, so that was it. Eunice thought I wouldn't survive, that I would come running back immediately. On the one hand, Bristol was big enough and far enough away for her to feel I would simply 'disappear', I suppose. Maybe she knew about the hostel from her legitimate fostering days, who knows? On the other hand, she expected me to fail. I guess she thought I'd be writing to her, begging her to bring me 'home' within a week. Eunice underestimated how determined I was, even though I was not yet seventeen, and how desperate I was to get away from her at all costs. I would do anything to survive. My freedom was worth fighting for at this point.

Eunice parked and, leaving Sarah in the minivan, walked me to the Waterfront Youth Hostel in central Bristol, where she dumped me: I was deposited like an unwanted package.

The hostel faced out towards the canal and new cafes and bars. There was a strange bridge in front of it, with big sculptures, and the place was buzzing with activity. It was all very odd and new to me. We stood awkwardly at the reception, where Eunice paid my first month's rent for a single room on the first floor. The place was brightly lit and clean and the staff were friendly. I was surrounded by young people coming and going, sitting and chatting on the bright green chairs or getting snacks out of the vending machines. I didn't feel part of this busy world and I'm sure we must have looked a strange, sombre pair standing glumly at the desk together.

Eunice turned and walked out the door. I followed her, automatically. She stood outside on the cobbles for a moment. I didn't know whether to hug her or not – she was never affectionate at the best of times. I suddenly felt extremely alone. But I couldn't show Eunice that, as I didn't want to give her any advantage. I didn't want her to 'win'. I was going to get through this, no matter what. I'd endured the most unspeakable cruelty at her hands and so, I suppose, I was pretty strong inside at that moment, albeit scared.

'Goodbye,' said Eunice. She looked at me coolly for a moment. There would be no words of encouragement, no cuddle or anything like that. 'This will start you off.' She handed me three pounds in coins.

I looked at the coins. That wouldn't go very far. I'd have to be clever.

'Goodbye then,' was all I said in response.

Eunice turned and walked in her frumpy clothes along the cobbles, then disappeared around the corner.

I was alone. Freedom. It was scary and exciting all at once.

I turned and looked at the canal, twinkling in the morn ing light. A boat was bobbing in its mooring near by and I could hear laughter. Two gulls flew overhead, squawking loudly, and I followed their path upstream and imagined it leading to the open sea: I'd worked out Bristol was a port from the signs in the hostel.

Although it was summer, it was a grey day and a bit nippy, so I turned back towards the glass door and went inside. This was my new home, and I had to make it work.

However, I was not prepared, in any way at all, for beginning my adult life alone. The three pounds was hardly enough for a bus fare and in terms of food I only had a bag of noodles, hastily pulled out of the larder. No vegetables, fruit, crockery or utensils to cook with. I did have an envelope in my coat pocket though and when I got to my tiny, white room, which had just a narrow bed, chair and table in it, I opened it and found a card signed from 'Mummy'. The red card was falsely jolly, stating 'You're leaving home' and 'Good luck'. So that was it. Goodbye to all that. As I sat on the edge of my hard bed, I wondered what on earth I was supposed to do next.

The Waterfront Hostel was in a fairly rough area. In the daytime it was OK, with students and tourists bustling about, but at night it was full of prostitutes, drug addicts, pimps, illegal immigrants, the footloose, the homeless, and drunken revellers. At the time, I had absolutely no idea where I was at all. I'd never been out for day trips on my own, I hadn't even been to Tewkesbury or Cheltenham under my own steam, so I was completely naive about city life. I watched the young people coming and going, dressed in skimpy outfits – clothes the like of which I'd never seen in real life – and they all seemed to be heading for nearby clubs and pubs. The Jehovah's Witnesses frowned on all this worldly, sexy stuff, and it had been deeply ingrained in me that going out drinking and wearing 'tarty' clothes was immoral, so I was intrigued by the apparent freedom and confidence of all the young people I saw out on the streets, clearly having a good time.

I realized, very quickly, that I would have to help myself entirely as no one else was there to help me. Eunice had let me loose in the world without any money to back me up. She didn't help me to set up a bank or savings account, no little nest egg, not even £50 tucked into my farewell card to get me started. Now that I'm a mother myself, I'm sure I would never, ever let a very naive seventeen-year-old go out into the world alone in those circumstances. I would make sure they had food in the fridge, basic utensils and equipment and enough money to live on for, say, six months. I would also have made sure they had contacts, a mobile phone, someone to call if they felt scared or lonely. The fact that I was simply taken to a big city and dumped there by Eunice is yet another example of how little she cared about me and how much she thought I was worth – that is, nothing. She must have told herself I was still 'evil' and would 'come to no good' and so abandoned me with the lowest of the low to struggle alone.

The first few days were very weird. I hardly dared to go out. I hid in my room, feeling very frightened. I didn't know how to talk to people or who to trust, how to get a bus or how to negotiate myself around the strange world I found myself in. It was really tough, but I had no alternative other than to deal with it.

I started talking to people in the hostel and met a girl called Beany. She was a young, streetwise, black seventeen-year-old with dreadlocks who had run away from home. She helped me to find my way around and we're still friends today.

By chance, I spoke to a helpful man who knew about something called Connexions, an organization for young, homeless people in Bristol. I was very lucky to meet him and I eventually found my way there somehow and they promised to help me find a job and more suitable accommodation. I had to borrow the bus fare back to the hostel from them as I had no other means of getting any money at this time.

I found getting on buses, working out where I was and understanding how to got from A to B quite daunting, but I managed it, after a few false starts. I was told by the people at Connexions that I had to 'sign on', which was very complicated, involving a lot of form-filling and hanging around in bleak-looking buildings.

I felt very scared at night as I got into bed, not really knowing where I was, listening out to the strange night sounds in the hostel – someone would be laughing somewhere, someone else was shouting, there were always voices gabbling in some unknown language or other – and, beyond that, the constant sound of traffic outside and a base beat thudding somewhere in the distance.

Luckily I'd been trained to starve, so in those first few hungry days I was able to survive on one plate of plain noodles a day cooked in a grotty communal kitchen. I drank water to fill up – another survival trick from my childhood.

One night about a week after I'd got to the hostel, I decided – probably foolishly, looking back – to go out and explore the area. Every evening I'd seen all the young people drifting towards the numerous clubs on the waterfront, all dressed up to the nines. They were like youthful Pied Pipers to me. I'd always loved music and when Eunice had gone out or wasn't looking I had sometimes managed to sneak a quick dance to the mini-radio, wearing headphones so no one else could hear. I had always loved moving my body to the freedom of a beat, and, because I'd been so sensually deprived, dancing seemed a really fantastic thing to do. Whenever I put music on and started to dance I would come alive and feel so completely happy in my body, released from the troubles of my mind, that I'd feel connected with my distant Romany and Irish roots. Nowadays, I still love to dance. I am fascinated by all things spiritual, and enjoy losing myself in ecstatic trance music. I'm sure that music, rhythm and dance are in my blood, rather than any evil.

The beats of the nightclubs were calling to me as I got dressed up in a hand-me-down sequinned mini skirt, black top and platform shoes. I put make-up on for the first time to go out (I'd bought some on one of our illicit shopping trips in Pershore and had experimented putting it on in secret). Finally, I responded to the lure of the music by venturing out, feeling very shy and vulnerable, but hugely curious and excited. I followed the flow of young people, who were giggling and chatting excitedly as they wove their way towards the clubs. I met some Chinese girls, who were from my hostel, who told me where to go. Around 9 o'clock I found myself in the Chicago Rock Café, where there was free entry up until 9.30, a bar and a tiny dance floor.

I made a beeline for the floor and let myself go, dancing away to my heart's delight. I loved every minute of it. The throbbing beat pulsed through my body, I was hot with sweat and with each move I felt freer and freer and freer, more liberated than I'd ever felt in the whole of my life. It was a wonderful sensation – utterly euphoric and exhilarating, and better than anything I could have imagined. *I was free! This was me, living my life, finally. I would make it alone. I would. I could.*

Around me there was a crush of young people, drinking and dancing, all having a great time. They were clearly used to clubbing – they had the gear, the money to buy drinks and they were flirting and chatting, like they belonged. I thought of how all these people had been free to come and go, drink and dance, laugh and have fun, all that time when I'd been imprisoned by Eunice, made to eat vomit, been kicked in the shins, beaten, throttled and had a stick rammed down my throat. Everything I had experienced so far had been horrible and humiliating. Had any of these young people around me been through anything like that? If I told anyone, would they believe me or would they think I was mad?

As I danced, and felt others moving to the beat around me, I felt 'normal' at last, doing something that any other teenager would do, any night of the week. But if people asked me, 'Where do you come from?' or, 'Who are your parents?' what would I say? It would take me a long time to work out how to talk about my life, having learned to keep my mouth shut and to be careful about every single word I uttered. I wouldn't know who to trust or what to tell, but for now, all I knew was that I was enjoying myself, feeling free to join in, unbridled and uninhibited, in a way that I had never believed possible.

Then I began to catch men's eyes and I to experience something else totally new: I was flirting. I'd been made to feel I was of less value than a piece of pig muck on the sole of Eunice's shoe, and that I was ugly (my hair had grown back a bit now, but was still far too short, and I hated it). For years, Eunice had made me feel hideous and despicable, and suddenly, as I danced, smiled and enjoyed myself, I noticed I was catching attention. So I flirted, and I enjoyed it. I moved my young body around and felt sexy – and it was great to see admiration in their eyes. I exchanged smiles with some men, and it felt wonderful. I felt attractive that night for the first time in my life, and it all felt innocent enough. The young men around me smiled – and I smiled back. It was simple, it was fun, and I was having the time of my life.

As I had no money, I couldn't buy any drinks, and anyway, I'd never drunk anything alcoholic before. I was just happy to groove in the clubby atmosphere and I was certainly in no hurry to go rushing back to my dingy little hostel room. After hours of dancing I finally sat down at a table, tired but happy, and watched people writhing about on the dance floor, getting more and more out of it as the night wore on. I was amused to watch everyone having such a good time. If things had stayed that way, I would have been content just to go home, exhausted, when everyone finally drifted away at dawn.

It's clear to me now that I must have been a bit of a soft target – a naive, young girl, out on her own, unused to the rituals and unspoken rules of club life. I guess I should have gone out with another girl from the hostel, or the Chinese girls I met on the way that night, and we could have looked out for each other – a lesson I learned the hard way.

I've had to piece together what happened next and my memory is still shaky. However I am absolutely sure, and would swear on my beautiful daughter's golden head, that what I can remember about that night did actually happen to me. As I sat watching everyone raving, a couple of Mediterranean-looking men in leather jackets and jeans sat down next to me and started chatting. They were then joined by another guy.

They bought me a drink, a bottle of blue Wicked, which I'd never tasted before. It had a weird, sweet flavour with a bitter aftertaste, but I swigged from the bottle, like I saw others doing, and felt very sophisticated chatting with these guys.

I learned that they were all Turkish, with dark hair, olive complexions and unpronounceable names. One of them had a little goatee beard, one looked like he hadn't shaved for a week (which I now know is fashionable stubble!), and one was pretty smooth-faced. They were all somewhere between twenty and twenty-five, and they were kind enough to buy me a second drink. I could now feel my head getting a bit woozy, but I carried on drinking, although I think I probably only drank about one bottle completely, as I wasn't used to it. They pressed me to drink the next one, but after a swig, everything went black.

The next thing I can remember is waking up in a strange bed with the biggest headache in the world. As I opened my eyes, I had no idea at all where I was or how I had got there. There was a naked bloke on the mattress, which had no sheet, with his back towards me. He seemed to be the man with the unshaved face that I'd first chatted to in the club. I lay for a few minutes, focusing with difficulty, trying to remember what the hell had happened, or how I'd got here. Blank. It was like looking into a black hole. There was nothing where my memory should have been. Suddenly, a fuzzy image flashed into my mind: I was sitting on some bloke's lap somewhere and being given a cup of neat vodka, which I tasted, and said, 'Yuk, I don't want that'. Then blank again. My mind wasn't working, and I couldn't link things up together logically. What had happened after I drank the blue drink? Where did I go? Who did I go with? Why couldn't I remember anything? It was like I'd been knocked over the head with a mallet or something.

As I began to come to, my head throbbing like a hammer, I realized that I was sore 'down there', but I was afraid to look. The bloke beside me was fast asleep so I started to sit up carefully. I was naked under a dirty old duvet with no proper cover on it. What was worse, the insides of my thighs were caked with dried blood. When I looked around, on the floor next to the bed I was horrified to see a bloodied condom discarded there. A used condom! I had no memory of anything at all, no memory of being kissed, of being naked or of being seduced. Did the condom and the blood on my thighs mean that I'd had sex? Had I lost my virginity? If so, who with? Was it the man beside me? Had I been forced? Raped? And what about the other men? Blank, blank, blank.

I shuddered, disgusted and fearful. I felt sick, not only at the thought of what might have happened to me, but from the alcohol. I had only had one drink, but having never drunk alcohol before I'd got woozy very quickly. Still, surely one drink wouldn't do that to me, even if I wasn't a hardened drinker? It wouldn't give me a total blackout, would it? One minute I was sitting chatting to the Turkish guys in the club, the next it was as if someone had pulled down the shutter on that happy scene and I'd woken up in a nightmare, in another completely different one. Blank.

Then another memory pops into my aching head: a room with wooden floors and plastic furniture – sort of blow-up chairs, blue blow-up chairs and a sofa. Again, I get the feeling I was sitting on some bloke's lap, but there's no face, no dialogue, no sense of who he is or what is happening. It's like watching a flickering film or half remembering something from a dream, where you can't quite piece the images together.

I kept staring at the condom in horror, completely mortified by it. I didn't want to pick it up, and pulled the duvet up round my neck, protectively. If only I could think, but my head hurt too much, and my empty stomach was churning.

Then the man turned his head on the pillow, opened his eyes and looked at me. He was definitely one of the guys from the club last night. In fact, he was the one who bought me the drink, but I couldn't remember his name. He looked at me blankly and all I could think to say was, 'Do you have a car?' He said, in a heavy accent, that, yes, he had a car. I asked him if he could take me back to the hostel as I had no idea where I was or how to get back to the Waterfront. He said 'No' and closed his eyes, ignoring me.

I now noticed that the walls next to the bed were plastered with gruesome porn pictures of women's vaginas, spread out for all to see. I was somewhat surprised to see so many fannies stuck up there on the wall, obviously ripped from magazines. They were very graphic pictures, leaving nothing to the imagination. I'd never seen anything like it before, and found it very disturbing. It obviously showed what he thought about women. What a nightmare.

I began to scrabble about, trying to find my discarded clothes, which had been tossed all over the place. My tights were ripped, which was strange, unless someone had tried to get them off in a hurry. I never would have done that, as I didn't have many pairs of tights – I would never just rip them to pieces. In any case, I couldn't wear them now, that was for sure, so I left them, shredded, on the floor. Once I was dressed, I asked the man where the bus stop was and he just pointed to some money strewn on the floor. I took about £2.50, then asked him again, now somewhat desperate, if he could take me home, but he just said no and went back to sleep, turning his back on me.

I made my way down the stairs of what seemed to be a dingy shared house. I must have looked a sorry sight indeed. I had never had a headache like the one I had that morning. My vision was blurred and I could hardly stand, let alone walk. Plus, I felt terribly nauseous. I staggered down the stairs to the next landing where a young man was tidying his room with his door open. When he saw me, dishevelled and confused, he said, 'Are you all right?'

I nearly burst into tears because someone was finally being kind to me. 'No,' I said, my voice wobbling, 'I don't know how I got here and I've got the worst headache ever and I don't know how to get home.'

He looked straight at me and said, 'They're trouble, that lot. You be careful.'

It was a bit late for that, as something horrible had already happened to me, obviously. At the time I had no idea there was a date-rape drug called Rohypnol which could be used to knock out and then seduce young, unsuspecting women and even men. However, I've since read articles about date rape, written by victims, and I believe that that's what happened to me that night. The fact that after one drink, I had absolutely no memory of what happened next until I woke up having been violated, with no sense of how it took place, seems to point to date rape. The terrible headache and memory black-out are also symptoms reported by a lot of victims as typical of the drug's after effects.

I found a bus stop and stood there, feeling utterly awful, my head hammering, trying to work out how to get back to the Waterfront. I had to keep asking people where the buses went to when what I really wanted to do was hide. I was sure my make-up was smudged all over my face, I had no tights and I looked like a whore who had been out on the game. I hated waiting there, looking so dreadful. When the bus arrived, I asked the driver if it went to the centre of town. Luckily he said 'Yes'. But as I teetered onto the bus I was sure that he and everyone else was judging me, criticizing me for being a loose woman. I felt like the lowest of the low.

Once back at the hostel, I crawled into bed and pulled the covers over my head. I had only eaten one plate of noodles the day before and I felt sick and weak after my ordeal. I couldn't work out how something that had started off so promising, such fun, had descended into something so sordid. I had loved the dancing, but somehow it had all gone horribly wrong. Perhaps Eunice was right. Perhaps I was bad and evil and terrible things happened to me because I simply deserved no better.

CHAPTER 19: *Mistakes*

I never went to the police, or told anyone about what I'd gone through that night. I hid under the covers for a few days, trying to piece together what had happened to me, and trying to heal from the humiliation and pain. I knew it was pointless to borrow money to phone Eunice as she would say I'd brought it on myself. I couldn't call Thomas or Sarah either – not only would Eunice not let me talk to them as they were still imprisoned on the farm, but also they were young, so what could they do? I couldn't contact any Jehovah's Witnesses because they would have disapproved of my behaviour. I had no idea where my parents were, and anyway, they had handed me over to Eunice years ago. So who was there in the world that really cared about me?

When I examined myself, I didn't think my attacker had managed to penetrate me fully, but I was definitely bruised and sore so he'd probably had a jolly good try. Perhaps he'd managed to satisfy himself while I was unconscious. Who knows? Maybe he and his friends all had a go while I was out for the count on the bed and they had fun stripping me off. The very thought of me being prone and naked, with him and maybe his friends attempting to have sex with me while I was unconscious was utterly revolting. I would never find out what happened exactly, and as I never reported it (how could I have proved anything in a court of law?) nor would anyone else. But I did worry that they would go and do it again to some other poor unsuspecting girl.

Some time later, I did see them again in a club; when they looked at me it was as if it was I who had done something wrong to them. It was bizarre. Yet they were clearly preying on other young women that night as I watched them operate. I didn't speak to them, but one girl I spoke to said they'd been trying to chat her up, but she'd pushed them off. 'They're only after one thing, those guys,' she'd told me, with some insight. Luckily she was more aware than I had been that first night out on the town alone.

But I had no time now to dwell on it. I simply had to pull myself together and get on with things because I had no alternative. I was hungry and needed money fast. I had to look at the incident in the club as a nasty 'blip' from which I would learn. So a week after the attack, and three weeks after being dumped in the hostel, I got myself a catering job and I found somewhere else to live. Connexions helped me find my first job as a 'grill chef', which meant I was flipping burgers over a barbecue. I started off at £5.25 an hour, then it was raised to £7.

I also moved into a rented room in Shirehampton in Bristol. There was a landlord on site and I had access to a computer in the living area which I had to pay for to use. I learned how to access the Internet and thought it was fantastic. The landlord made it clear that I couldn't have visitors back to the house, especially not blokes, but I had great fun at night exploring chat rooms. It was an amazing world to me; I'd had no idea before that such a thing existed.

However, within a very short amount of time the landlord started pestering me. He got it into his head that he fancied me and he started trying to control me. It was terrible. I was managing to get to work on the bus and do my job, which was fairly boring, but at least I was earning. But at night, the landlord watched my every move and in the end he switched off the Internet and wouldn't let me use it, even though I had paid for it. I think he must have been jealous of me contacting other men. Anyway, we argued over it and then he told me to leave. I couldn't believe it, but I had to find somewhere else, and fast.

My life was going from bad to worse, and I'd only been in Bristol a short time. But I was still determined to survive. I had seen what happened to other young people like me who had nowhere to go. Turfed out by parents who didn't love them, or couldn't look after them, they hung around on the streets, begging, prostituting themselves or taking drugs. There seemed to be drug dealers on every corner; this was a big city and it certainly wasn't kind, especially to lonely young people who needed to make their way.

As I was now homeless again I went back to Connexions and, with their help, ended up in a women's hostel in Redcliffe in Bristol. I got a job in McDonald's and, as I'd already had some catering training by then, I did quite well there. Again, I found it really boring, but I was used to kitchens, cleaning, sweeping and doing menial work, and I guess it did give me some independence. I had to get used to being alone, paying my rent, buying my own food, saving my pennies. It was a whole new way of life and absolutely everything was down to me, as I had nothing to fall back on.

There was a time when I was first in Bristol when I did let my hair down and tried some drugs. I also drank quite a bit. I call it my 'wild time'. I went out with Beany and some other people I met at the hostel. We were all in the same boat and gravitated towards each other. I felt I was learning to be cool. I think I was catching up on a lot of lost youth and, of course, everyone else around me in the clubs was doing the same kind of thing. I tried drugs like ecstasy and speed, but always with Eunice's voice in the back of my mind, telling me I was evil. I tried to ignore it and was discovering that away from her I was actually quite a feisty person who needed to let rip, to be free and make my own mistakes.

But I also found, after a while, that taking drugs didn't really do much for me. I'd take some and dance until dawn, and then feel awful afterwards. I never could drink very much (although I certainly managed more than one bottle of Wicked without forgetting what happened afterwards); I didn't like feeling totally off my face. I liked wine and cider, but hated beer, and I would try sweet drinks, like Breezers, which I preferred. In the end drink and drugs didn't give me the freedom I wanted; although they gave me some respite from the hard grind of everyday reality, they didn't solve my problems. I was still faced with getting up, doing a job, paying my bills, and finding a way to get myself to a better place.

It was at McDonald's that I met Braedon, an interesting guy around my age, who made a beeline for me. Skinny, with short, gelled hair and pale skin, he was very intense and sometimes funny. I felt sorry for him as he told me a long sob story about how his dad had kicked him out. He was very persistent and sort of attached himself to me. Within two days of meeting him, he'd moved in with me at the hostel. There was an attraction between us and he was fun to be with at the time, but I had no experience of relationships and, with the benefit of hindsight, I know I didn't love him. I was scared of being alone; I wanted someone I could call my boyfriend and maybe I hoped he would protect me as I was all alone in the big city. I'm not proud of it, but that's the way it was.

I had lost my virginity by now. After the attempted rape I did have a one-night stand with someone I met at a club, as I just wanted to get it over with. If sex was such an important thing and something every man I met seemed to want, I felt I needed to be in charge in some way. I soon discovered that men were turned on by the idea that I was a virgin, so the sooner I wasn't one the better. That way, I thought – mistakenly, as it turned out – I would be able to call the shots in my life. Losing my virginity, however, was neither pleasant nor fun – it was just messy and I didn't enjoy it. I had sex with several people after that, but I really didn't know what I was doing, and didn't much like it.

When Braedon moved in I was still only seventeen. Although by then I was a little more experienced, I didn't know what I was letting myself in for letting him live with me so quickly. I certainly wouldn't do that now. For a start, I was breaking the rules by letting him live with me in the women's hostel so I was jeopardizing the roof over my head. However, he managed to stay there undetected for four months before getting a hostel place of his own. I also stayed with him, although that wasn't allowed either.

In retrospect, I think Braedon just needed somewhere to crash and I was easy prey. I seemed to attract men a lot. Perhaps it's because I'm petite, or maybe it's my long, dark, curly hair (as soon as I left Eunice I was able to let it grow), but I've never had a shortage of men wanting to be with me. At that time I came across as very vulnerable and that was a magnet; I didn't seem worldly or tough like other girls, although I was probably tougher inside than most people.

I discovered that Braedon had lied to me about his father kicking him out; in fact, he'd left of his own free will as they weren't getting on. This should have been a warning sign, but I just thought it was better to be with somebody than be alone.

Then the worst thing possible happened to me. I got pregnant. We were using condoms, but something obviously went wrong. The thin blue line appeared on a pregnancy test and I was pregnant, at eighteen. What on earth was I to do? I knew by then I didn't love Braedon, and that I had fallen into a dysfunctional relationship. He had mood swings and would become suddenly very aggressive. Sometimes he would hit me, but because I was so used to Eunice's violence (which was much more extreme, of course), I fell back into the same pattern of taking it and not reacting. I didn't like it, but after years of conditioning, of being told I was worthless, it just didn't occur to me when Braedon hit me that I should call the police or walk out of the door. Part of the problem was that I didn't know what to do now I was pregnant and had nowhere else to go.

I was in a real quandary and I did weaken and call Eunice at this point. I needed to talk to someone and she was the only person I could think of. I was angry with myself for calling her, but being pregnant and alone, I felt I needed her help. It wasn't an easy call to make – it hurt my pride as she had already told me I was scum and would mess up, and now I seemed to be proving her right. As it turned out she was utterly useless and told me, 'You will abort it,' meaning I was a terrible person who would obviously get rid of an unborn child.

At that point, I really did wonder if I could be a mother and offer a child a proper way of life. I didn't immediately feel bonded with the little bean growing inside me and I did consider an abortion. But I also felt sorry for the baby. It wasn't the baby's fault that I had got pregnant, and it didn't seem humane to destroy a child through no fault of its own. I had always had an affinity with all living things and I just didn't think I could bring myself to kill anything that was alive.

However, falling pregnant suddenly made me think a lot about my parents. When you are going to have a child yourself you think more about your origins. What are you going to tell your child about their family history? Who will be their grandparents? Who will be there at the important times of their life, when they cut their first tooth or when they learn to walk, ride a bike, pass exams or even get married themselves? Being pregnant made me realize that I had to get back in touch with my parents somehow, but I had no idea what their address was or how to start looking for them.

I managed to get myself onto a register then for a council house and had to give two months' notice to quit the hostel when I was seven months pregnant. I was very unsure of what I wanted to happen with Braedon, but regardless, we moved into a two-bedroom cottage in Kingswood just before my daughter was born.

The birth itself was fairly straightforward, although I wasn't properly prepared for it. I never went to classes or anything like that. I was ten days late, feeling very restless and grumpy, when the first small contractions started. I thought, *If that's as bad as it gets it'll be a breeze.* But then they got closer together and then they were absolute agony. That took about two hours to happen. Braedon was in the cottage and didn't help me at all. In fact, he told me to go and get him a kebab while the contractions were coming. I went and got him his kebab, hardly able to walk, having to pause every time the contractions came and I doubled up in pain to get through them. When I returned, Braedon seemed more concerned about whether or not I'd got chips with his kebab than anything else. While the ambulance was coming I cleaned out my cat Pansy's litter tray and left Braedon instructions on how to look after her for the weekend – which he then completely ignored. I didn't feel at all relieved when the crew arrived, as I was worried about Pansy and whether she'd survive my absence. Braedon just sat there eating his kebab and watching TV as I was carted off to hospital to have his child. He never offered to come with me because, I think, he didn't really want it to be happening at all.

When I got to hospital I was already two centimetres dilated; they gave me some pethidine to relax me and put me on the ward. I slept fitfully between the pains and after about three hours, I began to have some mighty contractions and a bloody show. By then Braedon had arrived and was sitting beside me amusing himself on his PlayStation. He wasn't warm or kind towards me, and didn't help with my breathing or pains. I felt more alone than I'd ever felt in my entire life. When I rang the bell because I was in agony Braedon snapped at me to be quiet and not make a fuss. I couldn't believe his attitude, but I was in no fit state to argue. The baby was coming rapidly as the staff wheeled me to the birthing suite in a wheelchair and about forty minutes later, Ivy was born. When she was placed in my arms I have to admit that I didn't feel a gush of overwhelming love. I sat with my new, tiny baby in my arms and thought, *I'm in a terrible relationship, it's all wrong and I don't know what to do.*

I went home from hospital feeling pretty daunted about having a new baby to look after. I didn't know what to do and Braedon was not very supportive. I was tired and the baby cried a lot, so the first few weeks I just managed to muddle through. I was beginning to get warm feelings for the baby, but I wasn't yet 'in love' as people describe it. Then I had a phone call from a girl who told me Braedon had fathered a child with her. I had no idea what to do or say, and she changed her story so much I doubted it was true, but she was ringing me all the time and it was really unsettling. On top of this I was trying to cope with a new baby, who didn't sleep at night, and I was exhausted.

Perhaps because I was having such a tough time, one day in August 2004, when Ivy was three months old, I finally decided to track down my parents in earnest. I'd thought about it before, but hadn't known where to start and had let it slide. I eventually worked out that I needed to look up the electoral register. To do my detective work I went to Kingswood Library. Because I didn't know my parents' address the librarian told me to search on the Internet for family tree sites. That didn't help so I looked on 'lost children' websites – the sites adopted children use to find their parents. I drew a blank as I soon discovered that I'd never been adopted by Eunice. Then I tried the Cheltenham Social Services website. Looking at a map, I recognized the name of a road near where my parents used to live. I remembered the approximate number of their house and I wrote a short letter to every possible address in the surrounding streets, saying who I was and that I was looking for my mum and dad.

A couple of days later I was absolutely amazed to receive a text message from my parents, saying they would write soon and they couldn't wait to get back in contact with me. I was gobsmacked. Thrilled and scared at the same time. I wrote another letter inviting them and my nan to Ivy's christening. I was having a little ceremony, mainly organized through Braedon's mum, whom I knew quite well by then. It just seemed right to have something in a church, although I wasn't particularly religious any more.

Unfortunately, none of my family appeared at the christening and I was extremely disappointed, although it was a good day and I was glad that I had done it for my beautiful little girl. It seemed like ages before I heard anything further from my parents, then one day, the post arrived and there was a card from my nan in shaky handwriting. In it she explained that they hadn't come to the christening because she had lost her voice and my mum wasn't well, but they promised to send Ivy a christening bracelet, which arrived later.

I had written a little about my time with Eunice, although they didn't have the full picture by any means. Nan quickly wrote back: 'I have never hated anyone, but I'm afraid my views have changed. Something should be done about her [Eunice] as she can't go on telling such lies. Your mum and dad are the kindest people you could wish to meet and I think Eunice is wicked.'

It wasn't long before I took Ivy over to meet them, with Braedon in tow, and we re-established some sort of relationship. Although it was a bit awkward at first, especially as there was so much to catch up on, they seemed genuinely happy to see me, and kept telling me how beautiful I was now and how glad they were that I had a man and a life of my own. They were absolutely delighted by Ivy. My mum couldn't stop crying and hugging her and my dad looked pleased as punch.

After my first visit I received another letter from Nan, who seemed to be their scribe. She wrote: 'I don't think your mum has got over seeing you. They were thrilled after all this time.' Indeed, my parents started sending Ivy cards from 'Grandad Gilbert' or 'Grandma and Grandad', saying things like, 'Welcome to the world. We are so lucky you chose us as your grandparents'. From the little she wrote it was clear that my mum was wracked with guilt and my dad told me on later visits that she couldn't sleep at night for feeling so bad about what had happened to me during all the years we were estranged.

Soon after I re-established contact with my parents I received a huge package from them. In it were masses of cards: they had gone out and bought a card for every birthday and Christmas that they had missed with me (to replace all those that Eunice had binned), as a way of saying sorry. Both of my parents had written little notes in the birthday cards, saying things like, 'Happy Birthday, "Bright Eyes"', marking special events like my eighteenth birthday. They still feel sad that they have missed so much of my life.

Finding my parents and Nan again was wonderful but they couldn't help with my real problem: I felt trapped with a man who I didn't love, and who didn't love me, and who was becoming more and more nasty. Things had deteriorated between Braedon and me so that we were hardly talking. He would go out every day and only come back late, giving me no help with the baby. I was glad when he was out, but extremely tired – looking after a new baby single-handed was such a big job and one I wasn't prepared for.

The last straw came when I found images of child pornography on Braedon's computer. I found them by accident and was completely shocked and horrified. I knew somehow I had to get away for my precious new daughter's sake. Once I confronted him the relationship got even more abusive and after a particularly vicious row one night, when he tried to kick in the doors, I had to call the police. He was arrested and taken away and charged. I knew I had to protect my child and even now he is not allowed to see her unsupervised, by court order.

Once Braedon was gone, I felt utter relief. It was just the baby and me now. My six-month tenancy at Kingswood was coming to an end and I'd been offered a flat in Knowle. On the day I had to leave I packed up my few belongings, which fitted into a couple of boxes, and Ivy's toys. A friend came to pick me up and we bundled into her car. I was happy as we drove away from the cottage but apprehensive, too. I had to make a new beginning for us, but how would I do that? I was signing on and I was just about managing on the money, but I knew no one where I was going. Still, when I looked at Ivy's sweet little face as she lay cooing in her carrycot, I was determined to succeed. What I didn't know, as we sped along the road and I gazed out at red-brick terraces and leafy pavements, was that I was going to one of the roughest council estates in Bristol.

At first it was it was great to have my own place, a two-bedroom flat in Knowle. Ivy was about six months when we went there and I was still nineteen. The estate looked OK when I moved in, but I soon realized that there were addicts everywhere: crack addicts four doors up, heroin addicts across the road. Everywhere you turned, there were addicts and people living a very tough, rough lifestyle.

There was one particular neighbour, Cathy, who used to shout at me every time I left the house so that I dreaded any encounter with her. One day I was wheeling the buggy past her, on the opposite site of the road, hoping she wouldn't notice me. She was out on the front grass, her eyes glazed, dressed in a dirty sweatshirt and jeans.

'Oy, fuckface.'

I kept my head down and just kept walking.

'You're a slut, ain't you? How many men you had?'

I was terrified as Cathy swayed across the road towards me, puffing on a cigarette. I pulled the cover over Ivy protectively as Cathy blocked my path.

'Going somewhere? You're just a whore, ain't you?' Cathy spat and a huge gob of spittle landed on the buggy, which infuriated me.

'Leave me alone.'

'Oh, it speaks.' Cathy looked pleased at getting me riled. 'Off somewhere nice, are we?' She was moving over towards my dustbin full of nappies.

'Leave it alone.'

'Oh yeah. Says who?' With that Cathy tipped my dustbin over and the week's supply of soiled nappies, baby food jars, and other household garbage spewed across my path.

Laughing raucously, Cathy turned and sashayed back across the road, leaving me shaking on the spot. Ivy started crying as I tried to clear up the mess all over my little patch of garden. I was seething and scared, but I wasn't going to be beaten. Never again.

Every time I went out Cathy would be hovering, off her face. She'd call out things like 'Whore' whenever I went past. She just had it in for me. I was small and looked vulnerable with a baby in tow, so I think I was easy pickings. Other days she'd just spit and curse. She was always hanging around, looking out for punters, as I guess she was a prostitute. She also did drugs quite openly on the street, snorting lines of coke off the dustbins. I'd just keep my head down and hope she'd leave me alone. She was picking on me like a bully and I thought eventually she would give up and go away.

When I made friends with a nice man, Danny, from around the corner, who used to come and mow my grass for me, my crazy neighbour started abusing me again, shouting that I was sleeping with him. Then she threw a brick through my front window. I couldn't believe it. She could have hurt my baby, or worse, killed her. Luckily we were not in the front room at the time. I had to get the council to board it up and it took ages to get it properly fixed. I retreated indoors and tried to keep a low profile.

I felt very much that I was under siege in Knowle. It wasn't just Cathy; the other neighbours seemed to watch me all the time, and that reminded me of living with Eunice, being under her vigilant stare and constantly being judged. I found it very hard going, and I had help from no one other than Beany. She would babysit for me occasionally and I would go out to the club with another friend or two. But, after my earlier experience in clubs, I was now much more cautious.

I'd been alone for a while, learning how to be a young mum, when I saw someone I liked the look of on the dating channel on TV. He was called Colin and and he lived in Northern Ireland. Colin came over to see me for a week so we could decide whether we liked each other or not. I thought he was OK, but I wasn't in love. I hadn't yet fallen in love properly, and I wondered if I ever would. Perhaps the damage done to me as a child meant I could never give my heart?

Yet I had now bonded with my baby and my heart was fine when it came to her. Her golden hair, her little eyelashes, perfect fingers and toes brought up huge feelings of love and protectiveness in me. I'd had to learn fast how to look after her properly, which was difficult because I wasn't very organized. But I soon had neatly pressed Babygros warming in the airing cupboard and clean toys for her to play with. I also decided to add some animals to my family, as I had really missed my pets since leaving the farm. I had started off with Pansy (a rescue kitten) when I was first homeless and went to the women's hostel in Redcliffe; I now had five other cats, which, I think, provided me with the sense of home, of family and of belonging that I needed living in such an awful place.

Then Colin announced he was coming over to live with me. My first thought was '*No*'. But I still had no idea how to manage my relationships in order to protect myself. So he moved in with me and stayed for a whole year. At first it seemed OK, and to some extent it was nice having a man around, although, very soon, his behaviour started to worry me. First of all, he drank all the time and ended up going out four or five nights a week to the pub. I guess that was what he had done in Ireland and he was continuing to do it with me. I would get really wound up waiting for him to come home, sometimes at four or five in the morning, sometimes even the next day. I would think the relationship was over, but he'd come back and we would start over and lurch onwards somehow. I felt exhausted looking after Ivy and holding myself together, while under the constant scrutiny of my aggressive neighbours.

Then Colin went too far. I borrowed his phone one day and found masses of texts from women, saying things like, 'Hey babe, what's up? I'm sure we'll find something to do when you come up here'. I also found loads of photos of women's private parts and captions reading 'Sexy Jemma' or 'Dazzling Diane'. When I realized I'd been taken for a mug, yet again, I thought,

Right, that's it. I confronted him and he just said it was all his exes. I said he couldn't have that many – there were about thirty women's bodies on his phone. It was gruesome.

He left and went back to Ireland and then called saying I should send him a passport photo of himself for ID, which I did, although I think he wanted it for yet another website. When he returned we had a huge row. Although by then I thought I was in love with him, I knew I needed him to leave completely. I was a mother and Ivy had to come first now. I was still scared of being alone, but this relationship just wasn't worth it.

When he finally left I got my life back. I had been very anxious in the run-up to Colin leaving, particularly because I was so vulnerable in Knowle, what with Cathy's constant harassment, so it had been good to have a man around. Plus, my daughter had got used to him by then, although he wasn't her father. But I knew it was a destructive relationship and it wasn't going anywhere. All the time he was with me I think he was seeing other women and picking them up on his nights out in the bar. I was probably a useful stopgap for him, giving him somewhere to stay when he came to England. He certainly never played the father role and I never really expected him to.

Around this time Connexions helped me to get on a course at a Meridon College in St Philips, Bristol, especially for teen mums and their babies. I studied for my GCSEs in Maths and

English and after a year I passed. This felt like a real achievement as I had missed out on so much education. I had come away from Eunice's so-called 'Home School' with no qualifications at all, so I felt like I had finally accomplished something for myself. I knew that I would need to go further and do more in the future, but I had at least made a start. Plus, it made me feel that I wasn't stupid, and certainly, not as dumb as Eunice had always claimed.

In the meantime there were increasingly rough times with my neighbours. They seemed to be getting more and more outrageous: people were smashing my windows and egging the place just to amuse themselves. It was as if I was living in yet another prison, like it had been on the farm. If anyone came round to see me, I would be heckled and called names. My dustbins would be kicked over and my cats intimidated.

I did see another man after Colin, called Darren, who was a bit geeky and funny. I was twenty-one now and I went out with him a few times. He broke his arm on our first date. He was trying to show off and he bounced down a cliff edge in Brean and snapped his arm. I thought he was an idiot, but also rather sweet. However, I got the feeling I was not getting the whole story and in the end I think he was cheating on his girlfriend seeing me, so I just let the relationship taper off naturally.

My focus now was on leaving Knowle as fast as I could and I put my house in the newspaper for a council transfer.

Luckily, I found a nice woman who wanted to exchange with me. I went to see my new place in Lockleaze, a better part of the city, and liked it immediately. It was a much calmer neighbourhood and although the house was a bit grotty, I felt I could live there.

While I was waiting to move, my neighbours' treatment of me back in Knowle hit a new low when one of them came in and stole my TV, trashed the place and then threatened to beat me up. I called the police and had one of them arrested, as I had no idea what else to do. I asked Beany to have Ivy for a week until I'd moved; I was also scared for the safety of my cats and rang round shelters asking if people could accommodate them. I found a lady who took them for me, but after a couple of days she left a window open and they all escaped. I was devastated, as things seemed to be getting worse and worse.

I moved to the new house but kept going back to find my cats. It took a month but I eventually found them all. So Ivy and I started a new life with all our animals: Missy, Tigerboo, Biggles, Wolf, Pansy and Tinkerbell.

After all the drama of getting out of Knowle, I needed to find some peace. I needed just to live, to do my place up, look after my toddler and find my feet. Something I had learned was that being a mother was an important job, and it was something I wanted to get right. It gave me great delight to paint my daughter's little bedroom pink and make it as pretty as I could. I kept the place clean, and still do, as one thing I learned from Eunice was to hate dirt and clutter. If anything, I'm a real cleaning freak these days, up early with my rubber gloves and bucket. It's almost as though I need to scrub away the squalor of my childhood and certainly want my daughter to grow up in a clean and fragrant environment, not in a cess-pit like I did.

I also make sure she eats properly and have learned to eat more healthily myself. I buy fresh vegetables at the supermarket and we sit down at the table together and have nutritious meals.

So, now that I was in Lockleaze, living my own life, I was able to set myself up afresh and move forward once again. I had started chatting to someone on the Internet after leaving Braedon. We had been 'friends' for some time and he had been there for me all the way through the break-up with Colin and then Darren. He was very sympathetic about the horrific Knowle experience and knew that I was desperate to move house with a young child in tow. He was a drugs counsellor in Bristol, so he was easy to talk to, and I didn't feel I had to hide the truth about anything in my colourful past; most people would have run a mile when they heard what I'd been through. After a while, we exchanged more information, including pictures. I thought he was quite good-looking, but still only saw him as a possible friend. I had no intention of dating again and I was being very careful this time – I certainly didn't want to rush into anything fast.

Then we decided to meet. I have to say I found him very attractive, and although he was older than me Sy had a lot going for him. He was coming out of a relationship, too, so we were able to support each other. I think the attraction was mutual for both of us, and we spent many evenings just chatting when he came to visit over the next few months. Sy told me I deserved a partner who treated me better than anyone else had so far – something I needed to hear. Then we realized there was more between us than just friendship and we got together. We have been an item for about a year now, although he still keeps his old place as I haven't wanted to rush things this time.

He is so thoughtful and kind that I finally told Sy a bit about life with Eunice – as much as I could bear to talk about – and he was horrified. And when the ghosts of my past came back to haunt me, Sy was there to support me.

CHAPTER 20: *Justice*

The fact that Eunice was brought to trial is down to the bravery of Sarah. She was eighteen at this point and had spent the last four years imprisoned in a wheelchair when she was, in fact, able to walk. In desperation she confided in a local Jehovah's Witness – a man called Duncan Costello. Along with other members of the congregation he helped her to escape Eunice and they encouraged her to go to the police. To give them credit, they were prepared to blow the whistle on one of their own. Quite rightly, they didn't want people to think that Jehovah's Witnesses condoned Eunice's behaviour or that they would treat kids in such an appalling way.

Sarah called and spoke to DC Martell in December 2004. Once she opened up to the police everything happened so fast. I was amazed and relieved that the police took her story seriously. I guess because the Jehovah's Witnesses had backed her up, and finally, some grown-ups knew and really believed what was going on, something happened. When the police contacted me and asked if I was happy to make a statement to support Sarah's case, I said I was. Of course I was.

However, I don't think the police, or anyone else for that matter, knew what a can of worms they were opening. Or more like an ocean full of poisonous snakes.

Once I was began talking to DC Martell, in front of her video camera, it all just came spilling out. She was very easy to talk to, so for the first time I began to fully unburden myself of everything that had happened to me as a child. After all those years of being told to shut up, to not complain, to button my lip (or it would be split), now I just couldn't stop talking. It took a whole day for her to get my story down.

With evidence from the two of us to confirm that we were telling the truth and not making up incredible stories, the police were able to act.

Eunice was arrested in February 2005 and Robert was taken away from her by social services. Thomas was living with Eunice's mum and dad at this point, because Eunice had found him harder to control once he was sixteen. After Eunice was arrested the police talked to him too.

I later found out that Eunice's dog, Jet, had been left by her to roam about and he was found skinny with a manky tail, just foraging for food. She'd also bought a St Bernard, Sally, who was also abandoned in the garden. The house at George Dowty Drive was overrun with rabbits, and not looked after. And my black pigs Bessie and Bunty were abandoned at the farm and in a terrible state. The RSPCA found that their hooves had grown so long they couldn't put their trotters on the ground properly, so they had to 'walk' on their elbows. What happened to the animals was typical of Eunice's behaviour, in that she just didn't care about living things and would mistreat them rather than have to look after them. It hurt me deeply to think of the poor animals going hungry and wandering about, scratching around desperately for something to eat. My cat, Petal, had also gone feral for a while until some kind neighbours took her in.

It took two whole years before Eunice came to trial, during which the police gathered their evidence carefully, first hand. In the run-up to the trial, we had to be examined by a series of doctors and psychologists. Having my throat examined was absolutely horrible and more complicated than they'd reckoned on. Every time they tried to look in my mouth, or to put something in to keep my tongue down, I panicked and wanted to bolt out of the room. In the end, they had to devise something to hold my mouth open without actually putting something inside my mouth. To this day there are certain things I can't stand, like going to the dentist, because opening my mouth and allowing something to be put inside brings back all the old fear. Thomas and Sarah had clear scar tissue in their throats. My cleft-palate surgery complicated matters so they could not conclusively find scars.

We also had to have our feet X-rayed and a body map was

compiled of all the scars we had from cuts and grazes we'd sustained at Eunice's hands. These body maps were used in the trial as evidence. We all had many more scars than you would expect to find in a normally active child.

The psychologist listened to me for a long time and later wrote a report that I was suffering from post-traumatic stress, which explains why I've been having recurring nightmares. A typical one is: I'm back at the farm – actually, I'm breaking into the farm – and Eunice is outside on the lawn, in her red tracksuit, doing weights. It's a weird image and a scary one. There's a rabbit ripped to shreds on the lawn and I'm finding pieces everywhere, and a big dog is playing with all the bloody bits. Anyway, I'm inside the farmhouse, and I know I've got to get out before she finds me. I start panicking, and I'm running over the field, over towards the graveyard. My heart is pounding, I'm running and running as fast as I can. I've got to get away, but there's nowhere to go, there's no escape . . . I'm now a little girl and I see myself, running and running, over the field, hair flying. I can feel her gaze on me, her grey piercing eyes. I get hooked on a bush as I try to scramble over the wall and I can't get free, but I can hear her big feet coming, running after me, and I'll never, ever get away now . . .

Then I wake up in a sweat, shaking and confused as to where I really am. In fact, before the trial, I felt I was falling apart a bit. Events that I'd buried now had to be kept alive in my mind, so I could talk about it in front of a whole courtroom. It was like living through the horrors of my childhood all over again.

I found the process extremely gruelling and at times thought I was having a nervous breakdown. It was only because of the determination and support of DC Victoria Martell that I was able to go through with the whole thing.

The trial started on Monday 19 February 2007. Sarah was called to give evidence first, and then by the middle of the week it was my turn. So now I'm in my little room at Bristol Crown Court, waiting to be called to the witness stand. A witness support official comes to take me to the courtroom. As I walk through the doors my heart thumps. The court has old panelled walls, with modern carpets and chairs looking out of place. The room seems full of smartly dressed officials, the barristers and judge in their black robes and wigs, and it all looks terrifyingly formal.

What if she's there? What if she sees me? If I see her I'll be dead. I won't be able to speak. I won't remember anything, and within a minute of seeing her granite features, I'll know I'm entirely in the wrong.

I'm dizzy with terror as I finally take my place in the witness stand. I can sense that there are people in the gallery, watching, but I remember that DC Martell told me not to pay them any attention, to just look straight ahead and tell the truth, tell my story. I know that the defence will try and trip me up, make me out to be a liar. They will try to suggest that Eunice was a lovely, kind foster mother of the Mary Poppins variety, and that I was just a kid from hell, an unruly, difficult child she was forced to keep in line.

I look up to the packed gallery briefly, wanting to see Sy. I manage to pick out his warm, reassuring face in the middle of the crowd; the rest are all a blur. I lower my eyes and look straight ahead. I'm visibly shaking; I can feel my legs and arms are quivering in my smart new clothes. I fiddle with my hair, then with my bracelet. I have to do something to deal with my fear.

A chair is brought for me, so I sit down. An attendant asks me if I'd like a glass of water, and I say yes. The whole court goes quiet as the grave and I can sense everybody's eyes are on me, analysing my clothes, my looks, everything about me. My whole life I have been under scrutiny and it's just the same here, even now.

There is a curtain across the side of the stand so I can't see the bench where the defendant sits. But suddenly, there's a little rustling and I gather Eunice is being brought in. My heart nearly explodes with terror, but thank God, I can't see her. DC Martell promised me I would be safe from her gaze and I am. I hope. However, I'm expecting a big scuffle of some sort, because I can't believe she'd come in so meekly. I'm waiting for her voice to boom, or her shout to echo around the room.

But nothing happens. I listen out, very carefully, and all I can hear is the sound of people in the court shifting in their chairs, or coughing and clearing their throats.

It's eerily quiet, and I think, *I bet she's sitting there hating me, thinking of all the ways she'd like to kill me. I've brought her to this place and she'll refute every single thing I say, and then I'll be in for it.*

I glance at the jury. Every time I look up at them, all their eyes are on me, staring, like they're seeing through me. Apparently they could only see my head over the top of the rail as I'm so small. Suddenly, the court attendant asks me if I want to stand? Or would I rather sit? I indicate I need to sit. I don't think my legs would hold me. Meanwhile DC Martell's voice is in my ears, in my head, telling me to be positive. But I keep thinking, *If Eunice could get her hands on me she'd stab me now.* I can't get those sorts of thoughts out of my mind.

They bring me a microphone and the questions from the prosecution start. I'm so scared I don't even know if I can hear what he is saying. His voice is taut and sounds odd; it's like a fake tone – not a nice tone – a bit hectoring, as he picks bits out of my statement.

'So, Alloma, were you happy living with Eunice?'

What an odd question. What does he mean?

'Yes, I was happy, at first, but that's before things started happening . . .'

I try to be as honest as I can be. I can feel my cheeks are flushed and I can hardly speak. How can I start to explain the whole of my lifetime with Eunice, ten years nearly, in her so-called care?

'Sorry, Alloma, can you speak up? I can't hear you.'

I think, *That's not surprising, is it, because it's scary here. But also, how often have I been asked to speak over this past decade? I have been stopped from speaking most of the time, and this habit of a lifetime is a hard one to break.*

I imagine Eunice listening to me, grunting 'Rubbish', and looking grim, but I can't let her distract me now, and I screw all my courage up and tell the truth.

Then I'm given a plastic bag and there's a stick inside. It's definitely one of Eunice's weapons of mass punishment. This one has teeth marks on and I find myself wondering which one of us children the teeth marks belong to? It's splattered with dried blood and it looks horribly familiar, making me feel nauseated having to be anywhere near it. I grimace as I hold the exhibit up in front of the jury and I wince as I try to speak, but my voice hardly registers. It's like a hoarse whisper.

'Yes, sir. Yes, this is definitely the kind of stick she used to shove down my throat while she was beating the soles of my feet.'

I give evidence for two days. The relief after it is over and I've done it, I've spoken the truth at last, is enormous.

Thomas was on after me, and shortly after he finished, the trial was briefly adjourned when Eunice's dad died on 26 February, and on 7 March she was allowed to attend the funeral.

The media was banned from reporting on the trial as it was progressing, so it was only once it was over and I read the papers that I got more details. I read how Sarah described the first instance of cruelty she could remember, when she was four years old and Eunice made her eat dog fod, and then eat the vomit when she threw up. I read how Thomas described Eunice holding his hand over a hot plate until it looked like a 'gooey mess' and that he had compared what she did to us to torture.

I wondered what Eunice was thinking as she sat and listened to us Bad children, describing how she'd abused us. I knew she would show no emotion as the terrible evidence against her piled up. And as I feared, she said that we were lying, that the only physical punishment she gave us was a smack on the bottom, as a last resort. She said, 'I've sweated blood and tears for those children. I've worked non-stop to give them a good upbringing and education. I still love them.' She was always very convincing, but this time it didn't work.

On 20 March 2007, the phone rings. Ivy is sitting on the floor in a pretty little pink outfit with sparkly sequins, playing with coloured Lego blocks and chatting away to herself merrily. Missy and Pansy are snoozing in a ray of sunshine that's falling through my sparkling, clean windows. I'm on the sofa, watching her play as I pick up the phone. Panther-black Wolfy hops up on the back of my seat, purring loudly and starts nibbling at my hair in its long sideways ponytail, like he always does.

'We've got a conviction.' DC Martell sounds ecstatic in my ear.

'She's been found guilty of twenty-six counts including child cruelty, unlawful wounding and assault.'

I stop breathing for a second, before I thank DC Martell, wholeheartedly. To be honest, I'm a bit shell-shocked as I put the phone down. She'll go to prison for many years.

Ivy looks up at me, beaming, and proudly shows me a red Lego block.

'Look, Mama.'

'That's lovely, sweetie. You building your little house?'

By way of an answer Ivy goes back to fixing the red block onto a blue one and I feel sheer pride in my beautiful little girl's endeavours mixed with an enormous surge of relief at the news. I can breathe free at last. I lean over and ruffle Ivy's golden curls gently in the sunlight as she continues to play.

CHAPTER 21: *A New Life*

After the trial finished I chose to waive my right to anonymity and talk to the press. I felt that too much evil had been going on behind closed doors for too long, and it was essential to bring Eunice to book. Not her random Bad Book or Good Book, but the book of the legal system that is supposed to protect children in this country in the twenty-first century.

On 19 April 2007, Eunice went back to court for sentencing. The newspaper reports said she was as emotionless as ever. They also quoted Judge Simon Darwall-Smith, who said, 'It is difficult for anyone to understand how any human being could have even contemplated doing what you did – let alone with the regularity and premeditation you employed. You were careful to carry out what can be described as sadistic torture without being found out. This is the worst case of its kind I have experienced in forty years of dealing with criminal cases.'

He sentenced her to fourteen years in prison. She'll be

seventy-two by the time she gets out and Ivy will be seventeen – the same age I was when Eunice abandoned me in Bristol.

My main goal now is to get myself a proper education and because I've always loved animals I'd like to train to be a veterinary nurse. I want to work so I have the money to educate my daughter, so she never has to go through what I have gone through, in any way. I also want to buy my own house eventually and be financially independent. That really would be a fantastic goal to work towards and I intend to achieve it.

At Christmas 2006 I invited Mum, Dad and Nan over to my new place in Lockleaze and cooked Christmas lunch for them and Sy. In a way, I was attempting to bring us all together, to create some kind of family life. It isn't easy after so many years apart, but I did the same at Christmas 2007 and hope it will become a family tradition, creating good memories to replace the bad.

And when I have nightmares about Eunice and life at the farm, Sy is by my side. He is a wise, kind man who protects me and makes me feel like I am a good person, and worth something. He is wonderful with Ivy, a real father-figure to her, and we are slowly growing into a family. A loving, caring, normal family, which is all I ever wanted. I don't know what the future will bring but I am hopeful that we will spend it together.

Acknowledgements

I'd like to thank the following people: DC Victoria Martell, for believing us, for working so hard over two years to bring Eunice to trial, and for supporting us 'Bad' children throughout that period. The staff at Connexions in Bristol – without them I'd really have been lost. Becky, a kindred spirit and my first real friend. Corinne Sweet for bringing my words to life. My agent Ivan Mulcahy and my publishers Pan Macmillan.

Above all I'd like to thank my family, for their love. And Sy for loving me and my daughter; you know how much you mean to me.